WHERE THE REDWING SINGS

Booklocker.com, Inc.
2008

WHERE THE REDWING SINGS

Ed Kostro

Dedication

This Book is Dedicated
To The Children of the Earth,
To All Life Forms on This Planet,
And To All Nature Lovers
Throughout the World,
Who Believe, As I Do,
That We Must Help Preserve
As Much of Our Natural World
As We Possibly Can,
For Future Generations to Come

Table of Contents

Introduction

Where The Redwing Sings is a book of nature inspired poems and essays, written from the heart and soul of a life-long nature, animal, and wilderness lover; and it is dedicated to today's children of the world. I firmly believe they are the only hope for Earth's continued survival.

All one has to do is gaze about today to realize that our home planet is in trouble. Modern day life, massive urban sprawl, increasing industrialization, and the world's exploding human population are wreaking havoc on Earth's ancient ecosystems, and on her many diversely essential life forms; and far too many adults living today don't even seem to care.

It has truly become a very destructive, hustle and bustle, profit driven, modern day world; and very sadly, less and less of us are taking even a few moments of our extremely hectic, strife-filled, modern day lives to smell those proverbial roses.

Within just the last 200 years, we have felled over half of Earth's once vast old growth forests, and we have destroyed over half of her essential, life-sustaining wetlands.

Earth's oceans, lakes, and streams are now being grossly overfished, and they grow more polluted each and every day with our modern day toxins, industrial and agricultural chemicals, and garbage. And it's now fairly conclusive that global warming, horrific new storm patterns, and ever increasing world-wide drought and wild fires are only worsening the already dire situation.

Modern day urban sprawl, both industrial and residential, is also rapidly destroying Earth's remaining wildlife habitats. More and more of these nonhuman creatures have fewer and fewer places to live, and more and more of them are becoming endangered, and even very sadly – far too rapidly becoming extinct.

Earth's once sacred mountain tops, revered red rock canyons, and life-sustaining wetlands and swamplands are being decimated at an astounding pace today, and our once cherished and protected national parks and wildlife refuges are now being very callously torn apart - piece by piece by piece.

Unless we can somehow curb our seemingly never ending penchant for wide scale destruction, more and more animal species, and more and more of Earth's ancient indigenous plants, will soon vanish forever.

And there could very well come a day in Earth's not so distant future, when the only place a modern day child might find a wild animal on this planet is in one of our iron and brick, man-made, zoos.

Very sadly today, far too many adults, and most of the world's youth, have lost any real interest in the continuing study and protection of Nature. Most of us are truly products of our childhood upbringing and environment, and unless the children of today are once again mentored by nature loving adults, there appears to be very little hope.

Recent studies show that today's modern day children spend far more time indoors at their computer games and television sets than they ever do outdoors. But, can we even blame them? Most adults living today do the very same thing.

Indoor activities for all age groups living in the world today now far surpass former glorious outdoor pastimes such as hiking, fishing, camping, and boating.

Captivating old ghost stories are now read on a computer screen, instead of being told around a mesmerizing campfire in the deep dark woods. If birds are studied at all today by our children, they are studied via the Internet, instead of through a set of sturdy binoculars in the vast pine forest or on the sandy seashore. There are also far less stargazers these days; less and less inquisitive children request a telescope for Christmas.

We modern day residents seem to have sadly lost far too much interest in the magnificent natural world surrounding us, in its wild creatures, in the heavens above, in the truly vast and mysterious universe, and even in this very ancient and very intriguing thing we call – *life.*

If many of Earth's splendid remaining natural wonders are to survive into the next century, we must somehow immediately begin instilling a renewed interest in, and a genuine renewed respect for, and appreciation of, the entire natural world, in our children today.

Or very soon, and very sadly, this once great, green, thriving, vibrantly diverse planet will become an extremely barren and extremely lifeless, completely artificial, modern day world.

I truly believe that all of us must somehow strive to at least re-introduce Nature in all of its wondrous glory to our children and our grandchildren today, before it's much too late – for them, for us, for the animals of the world, and for our home planet.

I was blessed to have been raised by grandparents, parents, and teachers who diligently taught me the many merits of Nature at a very young age.

And with such an upbringing, I was able to joyously expand my knowledge of our natural world, and its immense worth, with numerous wilderness treks throughout the years, with continued readings of such writers as Thoreau, Muir, Emerson, Twain, and Longfellow, and with an ever expanding appreciation of ancient Native American culture and wisdom.

I still have so very much to learn about nature, and I truly hope that I will continue to appreciate, and to revere, the wondrous natural world that we have all been blessed with, until the very day that I die.

The poems and essays included here hopefully reflect both my ardent love of our natural world and my profound sadness at its mass destruction; and I firmly believe that today's children are Earth's only hope for tomorrow.

If even one of the nature inspired poems or essays in this book inspires even one modern day child to once again gaze upon something in our natural world with awe and wonder and respect, this writer will be a most happy one.

"Treat Mother Earth well,
And teach your children well.
Earth was not given to you by your parents,
It was loaned to you by your children."

An Ancient Native American Proverb

Where The Redwing Sings

"See a world in a grain of sand,
And a heaven in a wild flower,
Hold infinity in the palm of your hand,
An eternity, if only, for an hour."

William Blake

I arise before dawn's early light
And I journey to a favorite place
Here is where the redwing sings
He brings such a smile to my face

Since my very early childhood days
I've been entranced by the wet & wild
It is here, in the yet unblemished places
That I always wish to linger for awhile

Here is life in its very simplest form
Among bird, plant, amphibian, and fish
Here, in the wetland, they revere water
They know it brings life-sustaining bliss

Here, where the redwing blackbird sings
Here, where the lovely wild flowers thrive
Here, where the frog sings his nightly songs
Here, where earth's waters are vibrantly alive

As I perch here listening to this old wetland breathe
I can envision another lone human here centuries ago
As he too, enjoyed this place where the redwing sings
This place also bringing serenity to his world weary soul

Far too many today in our modern, hustle and bustle, world
Have sadly lost this connection with earth's life-giving things
In the last 200 years, we have destroyed half of earth's wetlands
This modern day fact, a deep sadness to my heart and soul brings

Today's modern children somehow have to reconnect with nature
Or within the next fifty years, our planet's wetlands will be gone
Please teach your children about the life-giving wonders of nature
Take them to a wetland, let them listen to a redwing's ancient song

Where The Water Meets The Sky

"I hear lake water lapping,
With low sounds by the shore;
I hear it deep,
Within the heart's core."

William Butler Yeats

Serenity for me has always been
Spending time on a wilderness lake
Here, where the water meets the sky
All my worldly troubles, I soon forsake

Here, where the blue water meets the bluest sky
I can silently drift along, in a tranquil state of bliss
Here, I can listen to the lake and to the forest, breathe
Here, in a place that whenever I leave it, I always miss

As I very slowly and joyously cruise all about this paradise
Listening to the lovely blue waters lapping against the shore
For at least a short time, it feels as if our world is still all right
It's a feeling of harmony and contentment, I shall always adore

Here, I can still leave behind the modern day troubles of mankind
Here, I can still enjoy earth's natural beauty, so very fresh and raw
Here, I can still envision how the Creator planned for man to live
Here, I can admire His glorious Creation, with reverence and awe

I would be extremely content to spend my remaining earthly days
Cruising along, looking and listening, to the sounds of this lake
Its birds and crickets singing, while a fish breaks the surface
And a loon calls out, in anticipation of tomorrow's daybreak

No matter where I may be now, on any particular day,
I can somehow hear these very waters, lapping on this shore,
No matter what I may be doing, at any particular moment in time,
I always somehow feel this place, deep within my own heart's core

Where The Wild Plants Grow

"We return thanks to our Mother, the Earth,
Which sustains us.
We return thanks to her rivers and streams,
Which supply us with water.
And we return thanks to all her many plants,
Which furnish medicines to cure our diseases."

A Native American Elder

I always love wandering the wild places
Those not yet destroyed by Modern Man
It is here, where Mother Earth still teaches
It is here, where I appreciate Nature's Plan

As I wander the thick, green, uninhabited forest
I soon come upon the ancient, tangled, Barberry
A plant so generously provided by Mother Nature
And used by the Ancients to make life more merry

After studying this wondrous plant for many decades
They found it useful as both a remedy and a decoration
They made lovely yellow dye from it, to paint their wood
Its beaded necklaces filled their daughters with much elation

Every single part of this plant, from its fruit to its root
Was used for countless generations as 'Great Medicine'
To treat everything from stomach disorders to rheumatism
Teas brewed from its leaves and bark, warded off infection

And today, more and more practitioners of Modern Medicine
Are looking to Earth's plants and herbs to provide new treatment
Yet, as Man now callously destroys more and more of her forests
Many plants have already been destroyed, gone their wonderment

I believe we could have benefited from this Ancient knowledge
But Man cannot wait to end everything that's considered 'old'
Today, as I wander the forest, gazing in admiration at wild plants
I wonder how many Gifts are gone, their glory never to unfold

※

In just the last 200 years,
Over half of Earth's old growth forests,
Have already been bulldozed away.

Who knows what miracle cures,
May already be gone today?

Mother Earth is the source of all life,
Whether it be plants, the two-legged, four-legged,
Winged ones, or we human beings.

Mother Earth is also the greatest teacher.

If only we would have listened far more closely to Her,
And studied far more diligently, and actually – learned.

My Beloved Boreal

"The clearest way
Into the universe,
Is through a forest wilderness."

John Muir

I have loved her since my childhood
She is truly a part of my heart and soul
I suckled at her loving bosom as an infant
In her arms, I hope to die, when I grow old

She is the enchanting daughter of an ancient god
Her father was *Boreas*, the ruler of the northland
And her beauty for me, is beyond all comparison
Her devotion to her children, so exquisitely grand

She provides loving sanctuary for 300 species of birds
From the woodpecker, to the loon, to the great bald eagle
And she also loves and provides for her many furry children
From the chipmunk, to the deer, to the black bear most regal

And the many lakes and streams and rivers under her domain
She has fervently attempted to keep so clean and clear and blue
In her lovely garden, she cares for thousands of indigenous plants
For all those residing here, her compassion and love is boldly true

She lovingly nourishes billions of woodland life forms
As she has graciously done for all these countless years
But mankind is now bent on defiling and destroying her
Which often now brings this forlorn child of hers to tears

Once her kingdom stretched from Alaska to Newfoundland
And once she ruled over a land with more than a billion acres
And once upon a time, all of mankind revered and respected her
My beloved Boreal, the Forest Maiden, we once considered sacred

❈

Every spring, for countless centuries, North America's vast Boreal Forest has sprung to life with vibrant color, pristine breezes, marvelous wildflowers, and truly wondrous sounds, as numerous migratory songbirds once again returned to her loving bosom.

First always came the robins, flashing their bright orange chests, and joyously singing out to her upon their return. Waves of warblers always winged in next, adding to this joyous spring symphony. These warblers, some having flown thousands of miles from as far away as South America, also soon began feasting on the rich bounty she always provided for them – millions and millions of caterpillars and fat juicy insects.

Flycatchers and northern orioles soon joined them, followed by hummingbirds, woodpeckers, swallows, and tanagers.

There were once thousands upon thousands of these magnificent songbirds in the northern skies, each and every spring, on their way to visit Boreal; and I, for one, always rejoiced in their wondrous return.

Throughout my lifetime, I've journeyed to visit Boreal in the springtime, each and every chance that I've had: to listen to her songbirds; to fish and swim in her very inviting and very invigorating clear blue waters; and to observe and study her magnificent wildlife.

Once upon a time, North America's gloriously immense Boreal Forest ranked right beside the Amazon Rain Forest and the Siberian Taiga as the largest forested area on this planet. Extending across the very top of the North American continent all the way from Alaska to Newfoundland, and from the frozen tundra to the green grasslands hundreds of miles to the south, the Boreal's 1.4 billion acres were big enough to hold 14 Californias.

And to me, ever since my early childhood, the Boreal has been a most gracious and most lovely hostess, as I eagerly and excitedly wandered her vast, lush, sparsely populated, wildly vibrant kingdom.

But very sadly to me, my beloved Boreal is now dying. The roar of countless jagged chainsaws and massive industrial bulldozers are now beginning to drown out the lovely songs of her children, and to eradicate her once vibrant landscape and magnificent creatures.

The Boreal Forest also holds vast reserves of both natural gas and timber. And to extract these commodities, large areas of the Boreal are now being grossly divided, callously torn up, and severely fragmented by huge pipelines and ever expanding service and logging roads.

Timber companies are now harvesting over 2.5 million acres a year from the Boreal, and over half of her forested area has already been licensed to logging companies for future harvest.

And very sadly, U.S. consumers - even those who are bird, wildlife, and nature lovers like myself- are responsible. Most of the oil and gas extracted from the Boreal goes directly to the United States, as do most of her wood products.

But even more troubling, and far more disheartening to me, is the fact that about two-thirds of the wood cut down in my beloved Boreal is now being pulped for paper used primarily to produce modern day promotional mailings and sales catalogs.

Seventeen billion catalogs - about 60 of them for every single U.S. resident - are now mailed out annually, according to the conservation organization, *ForestEthics*.

Most of these catalogs are made of Boreal's virgin fiber, and, in our extremely gluttonous, modern day, throw-away society, most of these massive catalogs go straight from our bulging mailboxes right into our overflowing garbage cans.

While my beloved Boreal is being murdered bit by bit, each and every day now, drastically reducing both the numbers and the quality of life for her once numerous winged and furred children - our enormous American garbage dumps and landfills – now overflow – with bits and pieces of her very essence – now so very heartlessly and so very callously reduced to 'junk mail.'

> *I have loved her since my early childhood,*
> *She is truly a part of my own heart and soul;*
> *And now, I weep for her modern day demise,*
> *Boreal, My Beloved Boreal, how I love her so.*

A Friend Stopped By

"If I keep a green bough in my heart,
Then the singing bird will come."

A Chinese Proverb
A friend stopped by this mornin
He often visits me in the Spring
A friend stopped by this mornin
Such joy to me he always brings

"Tsit, Tsit, Tsit!" he shouted out
As he perched there on my lawn
So I sat right down on the ground
For I knew very soon he'd be gone

This tiny feathered friend of mine
Was winging his way north to Alaska
He had stopped to rest and to chat awhile
His visit always fills me with wondrous awe

He had left South America several weeks ago
On a journey spanning nearly 5,000 long miles
And as I watched him resting here for just a bit
His determination and joy for life made me smile

We call this black capped bird a warbler
He's a 'Blackpoll Warbler' to be exact
Males of his kind always head up north first
Females always follow later as a matter of fact

And very soon he and his lovely mate will nest
And they'll spend the summer in the boreal forest
I love listening to and watching all winged creatures
These feathered marvels are truly filled with life's zest

After chatting and resting for a few pleasant hours
My tiny winged friend was once again off on his way
As I stood up and watched him winging his way north
I shouted out, *"Bon Voyage, My Friend, Have a Safe Day!"*

❋

Nearly 5,000 species of birds migrate every year,
Each and every Spring, winging through the skies;
We need to protect as many of them as we can,
To be their friend, and wish them well, as they fly by

And If You Possibly Can,
Put Out Some Food and Water, Too;
Spring Travelers Get Mighty Famished,
Soarin So Far and So High, Thru the Blue

And a Marvelous Activity
That You Can Introduce to a Child,
Is Identifying Types of Migratory Birds,
As They Rest at Your Birdfeeder For Awhile

A Magical Moment In Time

"Earth and sky, woods and fields, lakes and rivers,
The mountains and the sea, are all excellent schoolmasters,
And teach some of us more than we can ever learn from books."

John Lubbock

I was once again traveling due west
Arriving at the river just about sunset
My timing could not have been better
It was the most magnificent moment yet

The sun displayed a brilliant red hue
A slight chill permeated the prairie sky
An extremely magical and awesome ritual
Was unfolding directly in front of my eyes

Their numbers had been increasing by the hour
They had been flocking to this place now for days
The air and water now echoing with their vibrant calls
As the sun began sinking, I witnessed a magical display

Thousands of them circled all around my head
As they gracefully began swooping in for the night
What an exhilarating life affirming magical experience
And it quickly filled my weary human soul with delight

I stood silently out there now, completely transfixed
Beholding yet another marvelous wonder of the world
For me, a truly a magical moment in both time and space
And as it has for countless eons - all around me it unfurled

I had journeyed here to the placid banks of the old Platte River
To watch an amazing Spring ritual that's occurred for centuries
The truly magnificent sandhill cranes were migrating northward
And observing them here truly filled my heart and soul with glee

These huge birds would spend several weeks here on the Platte
Resting, feasting, and preparing to fly north as they always do
This edifying ancient ritual provided free of charge by our Creator
Had again worked its magic, ridding me of my Modern Day Blues

I now spent the entire evening perched on this muddy river bank
Marveling at another ancient wonder that so many take for granted
And as I slowly drove off at the first light of a wondrous new dawn
I wondered if mankind will ever appreciate the magic on our planet

Magical Moment II

"In the water, they have become the dominant species,
Though they acknowledge minds other than their own."

Heathcote Williams

My job had been driving me crazy
I had really needed to get away
So I soon found myself in Alaska
On a truly magical summer's day

The scenery here was spectacular
The air so very vibrant and clear
One of the last pristine refuges
A place, I shall always hold dear

And very soon, I was aboard a fishing boat
Pleasantly cruising a pristine Alaskan bay
As the Captain prepared the fishing gear
Up from the water it sprang, huge and gray

I raced to the side of our small vessel
It had surfaced directly next to our boat
It was a gigantic, gray, humpback whale
And now, right alongside of us, did it float

I excitedly reached out and touched its huge back
What a truly wondrous experience that was for me
Two far different beings, from two far different worlds
This electrifying connection had truly filled me with glee

And suddenly, this gentle leviathan from the deep
Looked straight up at me, with its gigantic left eye
Without speaking a single word, we had communicated
That moment will remain with me until the day that I die

As I stood transfixed, watching him vanish
Beneath the icy waters of the Alaskan coast
I thanked God for this wondrous opportunity
For a magical moment, I still treasure the most

And although several years have now passed
I always think of that whale, whenever I visit the sea
And as I silently gaze out at the deep blue ocean waters
I often wonder if that wondrous whale, ever thinks of me

A Place For Them

"To cherish what remains of the Earth,
And to foster its renewal,
Is our only legitimate hope of survival."

Wendell Berry

These creatures have a haven
They return to it each Spring
When they're spotted in the sky
Such joy to so many they bring

They begin leaving Argentina
Around the middle of February
They incredibly fly 7,500 miles
Their arrival filling many with glee

Legend tells of a very compassionate man
Both a nature lover and a Franciscan padre
Who saw a shopkeeper destroying their nests
So he invited these birds to follow him one day

He soon led them to the grand old Mission of San Juan Capistrano
Where they began building their homes, in its ancient adobe walls
Now, each and every Spring, they return here on St. Joseph's Day
Since this kind missionary had told them – here, was room for all

The Old Spanish Mission of San Juan Capistrano has now become world famous as the haven of these incredible Cliff Swallows, today's very romantic symbols for nature's magnificent birds.

In 1930, Father St. John O'Sullivan published the *'Legend of the Swallows Return'* in a collection of stories called *'Capistrano Nights.'* The story was told that after the town grew up around the Mission, one of the padres noticed a storekeeper angrily sweeping down the conical shaped swallows' nests, and chasing away these 'dirty little birds'. This kind padre took pity on them, and soon invited these very frustrated birds to the old Mission where there was plenty of room for them.

And these tiny birds have been returning to this old Spanish Mission every year, knowing their young are still safe within its old adobe structure. This was an incredible event marked by these kindly Franciscan Padres as occurring every year on March 19th, the Feast Day of St. Joseph.

Bird trackers eventually identified Goya, Argentina as these swallows' winter home, and the jump off point for their yearly migrations north. From here, as the swallow flies, the distance is 7,500 miles, and by the time they make their return flight to Argentina in October, they will have completed an incredible round-trip journey of 15,000 miles.

These cliff swallows have been observed leaving Goya at daylight on the 18th of February, in successive formation, arriving at the old Spanish Mission about the 19th of March. Most of the way, they reportedly fly at altitudes above 2,000 feet to take advantage of favorable air currents and tailwinds, and to stay above predators along the way.

A Tale of Two Rivers

"The face of the water, in time, became a wonderful book,
A book that was a dead language to the uneducated passenger,
But which told its mind to me without reserve,
Delivering its most cherished secrets,
As clearly as if it uttered them with a voice.

And it was not a book to be read once and thrown aside,
For it had a new story to tell every day."

Mark Twain

I had wanted to visit Two Rivers
For an awfully long time now
And it seemed like the perfect place
To take my winter weary dogs somehow

Although neither of them are bird dogs
There is just something in a canine's psyche
When they spot any type of bird - they're off
And of course, I can never keep up in my Nikes

Since Two Rivers Refuge is on the Mississippi Flyway
There were literally dozens of types of birds for us to view
And as my two invigorated mutts and I perched on the bank
Soon, all three of us were now filled with a wonderful renewal

We gazed in awe and admiration at bald eagles
And at ducks and intriguing white pelicans
We spotted sandpipers and giant white herons
And gaggles of geese soaring and landing again

A muskrat soon stirred nearby distracting them
And almost instantly they were off giving chase
And of course the old muskrat soon eluded them
And there was sheer disappointment on each face

But somewhere off through the vibrant wet fields
They soon heard a wild turkey's tantalizing gobble
And by the time they were done chasing after him
We were all extremely tuckered out and hobbled

I truly believe that my two exhausted canines
Enjoyed the Two Rivers Refuge as much as me
And I know we'll be venturing back there soon
Because it truly has many wondrous sights to see

The Two Rivers National Wildlife Refuge is part of the Mark Twain National Wildlife Refuge Complex that was established in 1958 for the protection of migratory birds; and this refuge complex spans over 350 miles along the mighty Mississippi River in the states of Iowa, Illinois, and Missouri.

And the Two Rivers Refuge (near the confluence of the Illinois and the Mississippi Rivers) is centrally located along The Great Mississippi Flyway, a major route for many species of migratory birds, affording visitors an excellent opportunity to observe numerous types of magnificent winged creatures.

Over 200 different species of birds visit this refuge throughout the year, and bald eagles are now common here in the winter as they gather near the open water to fish.

Herons and egrets are also commonly seen in these wetlands, and more than 5 million ducks, geese, and myriad other migrants and shorebirds fly through this extremely important river corridor during their annual spring and fall migrations.

The number of endangered American white pelicans passing through Two Rivers has also been on the rise. These white pelicans were especially captivating to watch as they soared high upon the thermal winds before coming in to land somewhere in this fresh water sanctuary.

Two River's bottomland forests are also used by various grassland bird species such as the meadowlark, the dick cissel, and the grasshopper sparrow.

Deer, squirrel, raccoon, muskrat, turkey, beaver, skunk, and opossum are all year-round residents of Two Rivers, and most of them are easy enough to spot if one takes the time to do so, and has patience and a good set of binoculars.

Since childhood, I've always known that plush uncultivated river banks are also a marvelous place to observe a variety of other fascinating wildlife – from muskrats and beavers and turtles to frogs and salamanders and snakes.

The Two Rivers Wildlife Refuge is also one of the few remaining places where the threatened decurrent false aster can still be found. This wetland plant, sometimes known as false starwort, is an ancient river floodplain plant species. Populations of decurrent false aster have drastically declined in the U.S. as more and more of our precious wetlands have been drained and converted to agricultural crop production.

I quickly decided that we would be returning to Two Rivers soon to see these endangered plants in bloom – before they very sadly disappear forever.

The Two Rivers Wildlife Refuge truly was a marvelous place to visit, for both myself and for my two adventurous dogs; but very sadly to me, places like it are now too few and far between in our now far too gluttonous modern world.

And very soon, if a powerful group of lobbyists and Congressmen have their way, there will be even fewer remaining wildlife refuges in the U.S., and fewer remaining unmolested sanctuaries for these magnificent migratory birds.

If you are as concerned about the future of America's wildlife, and its remaining wildlife sanctuaries as I am, I sincerely hope that you will learn how you can help to save them – right now - before it's sadly much too late.

Cathedral In The Pines

"I thank you God for this most amazing day,
For the leaping greenly spirits of trees,
And for the blue dream of sky,
And for everything which is natural,
Which is infinite, which is yes."

e.e. cummings

I awaken refreshed in the northern forest
On my very latest sojourn here in paradise
I already hear a most heavenly winged chorus
As I now gaze skyward with appreciative eyes

A wondrous natural cathedral rises just above me
I haven't been the only one to bow in reverence here
As I now gaze around me on the tranquil woodland floor
I spot their beds, a favorite sanctuary of white-tailed deer

As my eyes begin to focus more clearly in the morning light
I spy a timber wolf's tracks, his pious howl, lingers in the air
Then as I look at the trunks of some of these magnificent pines
I spot a black bear's claw marks, as he, too, had gazed up there

After giving thanks in this cathedral for another day in the wood
I begin to gather my belongings, and bundle up my comfy bedroll
That's when I unearth an ancient treasure, just under where I slept
The remnants of an ancient birchbark basket, several centuries old

Although religious groups call primitive men and beasts 'savages'
I'll take their simple lives, and their reverence for nature, any day
Others can have their modern churches, made of brick and steel
I still prefer this Cathedral in the Pines, and here is where I'll pray

"If the sight of the blue skies fills you with joy,

If a blade of grass springing up in the fields
Has power to move you,

If the simple things of nature
Have a message that you understand,

Then Rejoice,

For your soul is still alive."

Eleonora Duse

Earth Diver

"Remember that all things are connected,
And that all things have a purpose."

A Native American Proverb

This very majestic aquatic creature of the northwood
Is one of the oldest living bird species on planet Earth
It has roamed the world's waters for over 65 million years
And this fact fills my soul with both wonderment and mirth

The Native American Nations of the vast Great Lakes Region
Have numerous legends about this intriguing bird we call the Loon
I've been fascinated by this great 'earth diver' ever since childhood
I love listening to its extremely haunting and eerie, ancient tunes

Although I could never do justice to the old Indian loon legends
This is my version of one they've handed down through the ages
These ancient Native American lake dwellers respected all life
And in my heart and soul, I truly believe that they were sages

❋

In the beginning of all Creation
The world was a gigantic black void
Kitchi-Manitou, The Creator, made the Sun
And now the Great Darkness, He destroyed

As the new sun quickly rose out of this darkness
The Creator fashioned a bird that He made wise
And soon the glorious new sun's brilliant radiance
Began reflecting in the loon's now penetrating eyes

As the very first sunlight of this brand new world
Began to emerge from the once eternal black night
It soon began to distinguish itself, very distinctly
On the loon's plumage - now boldly black and white

Then Kitchi-Manitou, The Great Creator of All Things,
Gave the 'earth diver' one last extremely magnificent gift
His voice can still be heard in the loon's enchanting wail
Each and every new dawn – on the lakeshore – in the mist

Since I find this old Native American legend so very intriguing
I often journey to an uninhabited lake with my trusty fishing rod
But instead of fishing, I find myself captivated by the loon's wail
And very often, I do believe that I really do hear the voice of God

Theirs is the captivating eerie ancient voice,
I eagerly listen to in the early morning mist;
Their calls bring me such joyous tranquility,
They are truly one of Creation's wondrous gifts

Cruisin In Paradise

"I remember a hundred lovely lakes,
Opalescent dawns, and saffron sunsets.
And they have given me blessed release,
From my many cares and worries,
And the troubled thinking of our modern day."

Hamlin Garland

There is nothing like cruising
In the vast northern wilderness
With my soulmate and my dogs
To bring me such utter happiness

Mile upon wondrous mile
Of sparkling water and land
Nature still at its pristine finest
God's Creation, so very grand

No traffic or congestion here
No garbage or shopping malls
No urban blight or city smog
No fast food joints that appall

Everyday a magnificent adventure
Something new around every bend
My heart and soul always rejoicing
In a wilderness paradise without end

We have cruised for an entire week
Without a care, or ever seeing anyone
Just gorgeous blue water, wild critters,
Magnificent forests, and the golden sun

We travel for many miles
Upon pristine natural lakes
We marvel at nature's beauty
As each new dawn here breaks

We often stand in silent awe
On sandy, wind-swept shores
We wander in serene splendor
In tall stately pine forests galore

We gaze at ancient pictographs
Etched upon granite cliff faces
By natives who once lived here
Who truly revered these places

And here, wondrous animals
Still roam these forests free
Catching any glimpse of them
Always fills my heart with glee

The bald eagle, moose, wolf,
Beaver, osprey, and black bear
Nature's magnificent bounty
Has delighted us everywhere

Each brand new wilderness day
We cruise to a sandy new shore
And every new wilderness night
Another romantic sunset to adore

Sprawling round a blazing campfire
Each and every gloriously cool night
Under a magnificent star studded sky
Truly brings my soul absolute delight

The Northern Lights are awesome
The northern air always refreshing
A realm of pure mystery and magic
Truly one of Earth's Great Blessings

I sincerely hope until the day that I die
The great northwood retains its majesty
Because when it too is eventually destroyed
That for me, will be a heartbreaking tragedy

Earth's Many Wonders

"Everybody needs beauty as well as bread,
Places to play in and pray in,
Where nature may heal,
And give strength to body and soul."

John Muir

Rummaging through many of my travel photos
Has taken me on some magnificent mind journeys
I can't wait to head out on some more adventures
My heart and soul have a true wandering yearning

There's much I haven't seen yet
So many truly enchanting places
So many wondrous creatures
So many landscapes and faces

The world we live in and take for granted
Was truly created by a marvelous hand
And one really need not journey very far
To observe something unique and grand

And if you cannot afford a vacation
There is no need to fuss and fret
There's something quite interesting
Very close to your home I would bet

Perhaps it's a tiny wild wetland
Or it could be a sunny ocean beach
Perhaps there's a moss-covered cave
Just down the old dirt road a piece

Maybe it's a quiet little lake
Or a stretch of desert sand
Or a mountain top majestic
That soars high above the land

Maybe it's a very ancient, bird-filled forest
Or a golden meadow by a tiny babbling brook
Wandering through this glorious planet of ours
Is far better than reading about it in any book

A lovely day trip through a botanical garden
Can whisk your mind off to an exotic setting
And even at your very crowded city park
There's something marvelous I'm betting

Get out and enjoy Earth's many wonders
On your life's journey before it's too late
I plan to do this more and more each day
And my eager heart and soul can't wait

Wildflowers

"We are obliged to leave the country,
Looking as good, if not better,
Than we found it."

Lady Bird Johnson,
First Lady and Environmental Activist

On my many wilderness treks around this vast continent
I have always been a fan of our many native wild flowers
Wherever I may happen to wander, to camp, and to explore
I often stop to admire them, gazing at their beauty for hours

I have stood in awe in America's desert Southwest
Gazing in admiration at a wondrous Cactus in bloom
I've paddled a small canoe in the wilderness of Canada
Gazing at some truly gorgeous Marsh Marigolds, in June

I have knelt peering out at the vast Pacific in California
Surrounded by magnificent cliffside fields of Buttercups
I've hiked into the rugged Rocky Mountains of Colorado
Admiring the radiant Shooting Stars that thrive so high up

But for a nature lover like myself these very sad modern days
As I now wander here and there, looking for these wild places
I now often find that both our wildflowers and our wild animals
Are far too often being rooted out and replaced by parking spaces

Many people like me these days, want to help our environment
So many like me have started gardening with the future in mind

We plant native trees, shrubs, and wildflowers in our home areas
Which helps to attract native wild animals, of the wondrous kind

Recently, as I was searching the Internet to find flowers to plant
I came across an organization started by First Lady, Lady Bird
I found it a marvelous place to research native plants and flowers
Please plant your garden with the future in mind; read her words:

> ***"We are obliged to leave the country,***
> ***Looking as good,***
> ***If not better,***
> ***Than we found it."***

Her website is *The Wildflower Center*
And it contains a marvelous database,
Spanning Different Areas of the U.S. and Canada,
Of Over 17,000 Native Plants and Flowers,
And Some Truly Outstanding Photography.
And, there are many other
Wildflower and Native Plant Resources
In Every Geographic Area of North America.

Are You Searching
For Ways to Help Restore
Our Once Beautiful Continent?

Planting A Few Native
Wildflowers,
Shrubs, or Trees,
In Your Own Backyard,
Just Might Help a Little.

Native Plants, and Flowers, and Trees, and Shrubs,
Usually Thrive in Their Own Natural Environments;
They Also Attract Wondrous Native Birds and Animals.

Red Rock Dawn

"There is a way that nature speaks,
That the land speaks.
Most of the time we are simply not patient enough,
Or quiet enough, to pay attention to the story."

Linda Hogan

I awaken very slowly to the soothing silence
Of an extremely majestic red rock canyon morn
I am once again very happily roaming the wild
A place where my soul always seems to be reborn

As I look off to the distant, brightening horizon
I soon envision a band of spirits now drawing near
They seem to be diligently scouring the landscape
Perhaps searching for a jack rabbit, or a mule deer

Suddenly, a deer does break the canyon silence
As I watch him scamper off through a steep ravine
And then I spy this group of very shadowy ancients
Rushing after him in the dawn's now mystical gleam

I soon watch in my now completely spellbound state
As they return and triumphantly march down the hill
They are definitely an exhilarating spectacular sight
Their eerie spirit presence has given me such a thrill

I soon huddle at the black ash-scarred rock laden circle
Of their now brilliantly glowing and magical campfire
I can feel their undying love for this ancient rugged land
And I can somehow sense in them a truly everlasting desire

Soon they begin chanting and playing their ancient instruments
Very melodic sounds now loudly echoing off these jagged walls
And now I'm totally entranced by their mystifying flute melodies
Their extremely captivating native flute music truly does enthrall

Long ago they had roamed these red rock canyons
A simple and proud people and so very joyously free
As I prepare to head off on my own canyon adventure
My heart and soul are now completely immersed in glee

Who knows what ancient artifacts and treasures
That I might curiously unearth on this land today
Who knows what other traces of these long ago lives
I might run across as I excitedly wander off on my way

I had awakened very slowly and quite enchantingly
To an extremely exhilarating red rock canyon morn
And soon, I was somehow reliving their ancient history
In a place where my soul had now been magically reborn

Hoodoo

The Legend of Bryce Canyon,
As Explained to a Park Naturalist in 1936,
By a Paiute Indian Elder

A very long, long, long, time ago
The Legend People lived in this place
There were a very great many of them
They did not belong to the human race

They had enormous supernatural powers
They wisely ruled this very ancient land
They were called the *To-when-an-ung-wa*
They were magnificent beings most grand

They would sit in sage, lengthy councils
Pontificating about life and all of creation
They could fly, speak, and even shape shift
Theirs was truly a wondrous, peaceful nation

They dressed as colorful plumed birds and furry animals
Or as great lizards and wise snails, and other such things
But eventually, these Legend People came to be very evil
Soon their terrible misdeeds, disaster to them would bring

You can still see them in this ancient place today
Still standing in long rows, and some sitting down
Some of them still desperately clinging to one another
And each of them, now wearing enormous immortal frowns

One sad day, they began to fight and even to hate one another
And horrifically, they even began to steal and to cheat and lie
So one night, in disgust, Coyote turned them all into red stone
And here at night, in the moonlight, you can still hear them cry

**"The name of this place is Angka-ku-wass-a-wits
(Red Painted Faces),
And this is the story the people tell."**

❋

Bryce Canyon National Park covers almost 36,000 acres in southern Utah, and it is truly a magical and mystical place; a place where one's imagination can easily run wild.

This park is known for its numerous eerie, red-faced, 'Hoodoos,' or tall thin rock spires, which obviously inspired this fascinating Paiute Indian Legend.

If you stand in the canyon long enough, peering at these odd shaped Hoodoos, you can actually see many different images and frozen facial expressions embedded in these ancient stones – and you can quickly realize how this legend came to be.

Bryce Canyon was designated as a protected National Park in 1928. It is named after pioneer Ebenezer Bryce, who arrived here in this vast surreal landscape with his family in 1875. His famous quote: *"This is a hell of a place to lose a cow."*

Today, one enters this magnificent national park at an elevation of 6,600 feet. At the end of its spectacular and very awe inspiring 18-mile spiraling road, the elevation rises to 9,105 feet.

Geologists say that Bryce Canyon was once filled with numerous lakes and streams, but as time passed, huge sediment deposits collected in these bodies of water, causing them to eventually dry up, and leaving behind these very mysterious and truly captivating red sandstone Hoodoos.

I've journeyed to Bryce Canyon many times over the years, and I always find something new and intriguing and mystifying here.

And I truly like the Paiute Indian version of how Bryce Canyon came to be much better than the scientific one.

He Brings The Sun

"When piped a tiny voice hard by,
Gay and polite, a cheerful cry,
Chic-chic-a-dee-dee! Saucy note,
Out of sound heart and merry throat."

Ralph Waldo Emerson

A tiny friend just came a calling
At my window bird feeding station
And he delightfully brought with him
Memories filled with sunny warm elation

He very merrily called out as if to remind me
Of the many bright sunny days that I have spent
Wandering through the forests and the meadows
So eagerly following the lyrical trail that he's sent

There is nothing quite as exhilarating
As embarking on a stroll in the woods
And suddenly hearing him calling out
As only this tiny feathered friend could

"Chick-a-dee-dee-dee!"
Is his very merry song
"Come-follow-me!"
It never takes me very long

I always forget about my problems
As I eagerly traipse right after him

And he seems to enjoy this game of tag
As he slowly flutters above me in the wind

Eventually he leads me to a fine group
Of his feathered brethren, now at rest
And I soon stop and marvel at them too
Since he always leads me to the very best

There before my eager eyes
I can usually excitedly see
All sorts of winged creatures
Huddled together in the trees

Woodpeckers and hatches
House wrens and titmice
Cardinals and swallows
All gathered quite nice

My tiny friend acts as a nucleus
Who brings kindred souls together
We all seem comforted by his presence
In even the nastiest of northwood weather

And when he learns to trust you
And he knows you're not a threat
He might lead you to a wise old owl
Dozing peacefully just above your head

He is brave and playful and smart
And a most wondrous little creature
And keeping everyone's soul warm
Seems to be his divinely given feature

"Chick-a-dee-dee-dee!"
Is a song I hold dear to my heart
And as soon as I possibly can
I always follow after it like a dart

"I promise I'll come follow you today!"
I soon shout out to my feathered friend
And he nods his tiny head before departing
As if this sunny little creature comprehends

Lady Of The Lake

*"I realized that if I had to choose,
I would rather have birds than airplanes."*

Charles Lindbergh

I will have to admit
I am enthralled by her
She has so many charms
She's such a captivating girl

She's the Lady of the Lake
And she has captured my heart
Her beauty is quite mesmerizing
In the ways of the wild she is smart

I've been watching her ready her home
High atop a magnificent white pine tree
And she's gotten used to me peering at her
She seems to have accepted my total curiosity

And now that her cozy nest is ready
Soon her tiny children will be born
And I really hope I'm around that day
It will be a wondrous northwood morn

I love watching her fishing with such skill
The Lady of the Lake truly fills me with glee
And I've decided to call her 'Lady Norwood'
Some call her a Fish Hawk - this lovely Osprey

The osprey is a large raptor with a wingspan of 4-6 feet, and a weight of approximately 4 pounds. It has a dark brown back and a white belly, as well as a white head, which features a dark stripe running from its yellow eyes to the back of its head. Female ospreys are slightly larger than males.

These extremely captivating birds winter in Florida, in the Caribbean, on the Gulf Coast, and in South America. And thankfully, many of them still summer in the great northwood, usually on or near a body of water.

They dine almost exclusively on fish, often catching their meals by hovering over the water at an altitude of up to 200 feet, then rapidly diving feet-first into the icy water to catch their prey. I've always been fascinated watching them fish. They have reversible front toes, as well as sharp barbs, called 'spicules,' which help them hold onto a slippery fish while in flight. Normally, an osprey will aerodynamically position a fish head-first in its sharp talons before returning to its nest.

I've also always been fascinated watching the raucous seagulls chasing after an osprey with a freshly caught fish, hoping the osprey will drop it. But these birds seldom do, especially when they are devoted mothers returning to the nest to feed their young.

Like bald eagles, ospreys often reuse old nests, adding fresh material to them each season, and they prefer nests near lakes and streams.

The female osprey usually lays three eggs, which hatch in about 4 to 5 weeks, and after about 10 weeks, the young will have their flight feathers.

The female osprey diligently stays on the nest the majority of this time, with the male giving Mom an occasional break when she leaves to hunt for food.

Like many birds of prey, the osprey suffered terribly during the 1960s and 70s due to the rampant use of DDT and other dangerous pesticides. Scientific research laid the foundation for Rachel Carson's classic book, *Silent Spring*, which alerted us to the fact that DDT was working its way up the food chain and horrendously thinning the eggs of these birds.

Fortunately for this Lady of the Lake, and for others of her kind, DDT was banned in the U.S. in 1972, and thanks to the extremely hard work of many dedicated people, these magnificent winged creatures are beginning to finally make a rebound.

Lady Of The Wood

"Beneath you birch with silver bark
And boughs so pendulous and fair,
The brook falls scattered down the rock:
and all is mossy there."

Samuel Taylor Coleridge

She has always captivated me
This Noble Lady of the Wood
She is very lovely and maternal
Her domain so magical and good

She is always first in a new forest
When the old is destroyed by men
She has the wisdom and the fortitude
To start an entire new woodland again

She provides sanctuary for many insects
Many woodland creatures call her home
She was revered by ancient forest people
And has been the subject of many a poem

Her bark and leaves were used as medicine
She provided toboggans and baby cradles too
Her sweet flowing sap was used to make syrup
And many a fisherman enjoyed her sturdy canoe

She has helped to fill our forests with enchanting music
From her wondrous gift, ancient craftsmen made a drum
Each evening in the woodland, I can still hear the echoes
Of her ancient melodies, joyous dancing, and glorious fun

And each and every time that I journey north to visit her
I spot some of her many children living out on the prairie
I can always tell where an early settler's old farmhouse stood
Pioneers knew this lovely lady helped to make their lives merry

She somehow always captivates me,
This Ancient Noble Lady of the Wood;
She's extremely lovely and very maternal,
Lady Birch's domain, so magical and good

Night Wing

"The caged bird sings with a fearful trill
Of things unknown but longed for still;
And his tune is heard on the distant hill,
For the caged bird, sings of freedom."

Maya Angelou

Northwood nights are magical
If only I give in and let them be
Moonlight provides the answer
As it somehow sets my soul free

I perch on the lush bank
Of this ancient silent lake
I gaze at the moonlit water
There is nary a rippled wake

I look to the many stars
In the vast heavens above
I marvel at all His Creation
Provided so freely with love

I study the night raptor
Gliding so high in the sky
Then I slowly close my eyes
As my soul now attempts to fly

I soon become this bird
If only in my mind's eye
And magically I'm content
Now being one of its kind

I feel no hatred, greed, or malice
Or any need to dominate this land
Simply being just a small part of it
My winged soaring soul feels grand

Suddenly I hear the many crickets
Singing their sweet nightly lullaby
Soon I hear captivating lake ripples
As the spirit of the breeze passes by

Then I hear a distant black and white loon
It's now very lovingly calling out to its mate
They will soon cuddle here in this moonlight
For tomorrow's dawn, together they will wait

I then gaze down upon these tall pines
Standing vigil along this ancient shore
And the view from this very lofty angle
Is one that my soaring spirit now adores

These days I often find myself
Circling my new world all night
And when the dawn finally arrives
My soul sings gloriously at first light

Now I watch the dawn's spirit awakening
As it does each and every brand new day
Then I slowly descend and shed my wings
And now, I'm content to journey on my way

As I once again wander through this forested realm
I marvel at all the serenity my northwood nights bring
If our immortal souls are truly capable of reincarnation
I now yearn to be a simple and free creature with wings

Northwood Days

*"An early morning walk,
Is a blessing,
For the entire day."*

Henry David Thoreau

A beam of sunlight peeks
Across the northwood sky
I soon hear the robin's song
What a pure joy it is to rise

I throw open the log cabin window
The northwood air so fresh and clean
A new day to enjoy nature's marvels
So many natural sights yet to be seen

With my eager dogs at my side
I once again soon rush outdoors
To a northwood bird symphony
I simply can't wait to hear more

As the sunlight quickly approaches
Many wonders lay before our eyes
My four dogs eagerly begin to romp
I marvel at glistening northwood skies

Soon we quickly saunter down
To the rickety old wooden dock
All of us joyously diving into the lake
What an eye opening life affirming shock

A very large painted turtle
And a mallard now glide by
An osprey fishes for breakfast
A bald eagle soars through the sky

A familiar green northwood trail
Soon beckons to my heart and soul
So my canine companions and I dry off
And through the woods we all now eagerly go

The gigantic oak, pine, birch, and maple trees
Each now basking in the sun's life giving rays
We follow our tiny feathered friend, the chickadee
As he merrily guides us along the green forested trail

Another red robin soon merrily sings out
As I watch an industrious black ant crawl
A hungry woodpecker now loudly thumps
As a tiny chipmunk merrily calls out to us all

The loons are all now happily swimming
A raucous black raven caws out in utter joy
I skip rocks across the serene lake surface
Feeling just like an inquisitive young boy

Purple wildflowers are all now in bloom
I eagerly pick a fresh bouquet for my wife
Then I perch by this magnificent lakeshore
To observe all this rich natural god-given life

I sit very serenely with my faithful dogs
For hours by the northwood lake's bank
Marveling at Earth's splendid Creation
And in my heart and soul giving thanks

A beam of sunlight had peeked,
Across the vast northwood sky;
And soon I heard a robin's song,
What a joy here, just to be alive

Rainy Day Lullaby

"Let the rain kiss you.
Let the rain beat upon your head with silver liquid drops.
Let the rain, sing you a lullaby."

Langston Hughes

A rainy day in the northwood
Can truly be a most magical thing
I took a long walk in the woods yesterday
And what a marvelous experience it did bring

The huge vibrant muddy puddles were spectacular
The soft pitter patter of the raindrops in the pine trees
The very wondrous sight of a doe and her newborn fawn
The hint of a spectacular summer about to arrive in the breeze

The gorgeous wildflowers seemed to be enjoying the rain
The songbirds gathered in the trees were chirping a lullaby
As I walked on drenched in the earth's splendid elixir of life
I suddenly reached the lakeshore and soon peered into the sky

And as I stood on the northwood lakeshore taking it all in
The glorious sun broke through the clouds off to the west
As I stood watching yet another wondrous miracle of nature
I knew tomorrow would dawn brightly and now I felt blessed

Then suddenly from nowhere right in front of me
A magnificent loon called out and glided right by
He too seemed to sense the magic in this moment
His song capped off a marvelous northwood lullaby

Langston Hughes' words now echoed in my head
As I stood there transfixed, joyously taking it all in:

Let earth's blessed rain kiss you,
Let the rain beat down from the sky;
Let the magnificence of nature sing you,
An absolutely glorious rainy day lullaby

Orb of Day

"With zealous step he climbs the upland lawn,
And bows in homage to the rising dawn;
Imbibes with eagle eye the golden ray,
And watches as it moves the orb of day."

Erasmus Darwin

In the very hot days of summer
I rise and head out before dawn
I take my trusty binoculars with me
To observe life here on Earth's lawn

I silently perch on my favorite hill
Just listening and peering all around
Sunrise brings many wondrous treasures
And each new day, so many here abound

I usually hear a distant rooster
He's already ascended his throne
He loves singing his morning song
And now, the world is again his own

I see the early bird pluck that worm
I watch a very industrious ant haul
A woodpecker thumps very loudly
A fuzzy caterpillar begins to crawl

A catfish playfully jumps in the pond
I hear a mourning dove devoutly pray
A newborn bird cries out for breakfast
A wise old donkey now begins to bray

A horse gallops joyously in a distant field
I spot a black and white cow chewing cud
A very lovely blue butterfly starts fluttering
A wondrous dragonfly buzzes by in the mud

A baby sparrow gets its first flying lesson
A brown chipmunk now so merrily chatters
A red-tailed hawk soars so very high above
An old grey squirrel so very eagerly gathers

As I peer off towards the dark green forest
I soon spot a white-tailed deer and her fawn
As the heat of the day now begins to descend
I'm once again at peace on this summer's dawn

I look down towards my home and garden
These days, it's the place I am content to be
So I pick a few purple wildflowers for my wife
A gift of nature that truly fills her heart with glee

I then head back down the path to begin my day
Feeling just a tad better about this mad old world
For myself, in these extremely hot days of summer
Nothing calms, like watching the orb of day unfurled

Sanctuary

"In every walk with nature,
One receives far more than he seeks."

John Muir

When life's gotten me down
And I now need to rejuvenate
I often take a leisurely stroll here
In a kingdom still serenely sedate

Here I still find a blissful realm
That is both peaceful and serene
Here I still find a secluded sanctuary
Soothingly painted a wondrous green

The air is still fresh and sweet
Lovely melodies here truly please
Very blissful tranquility and harmony
Magically drift in on the fragrant breeze

No bickering or quarreling here
No petty nonsense or city noise
No outside worldly interferences
No modern distractions to annoy

No very ghastly television news stories
No horrid reports of more war and crime

Residents here follow God's natural order
Leading a life that is usually quite sublime

While just outside this small forested realm
The rest of the world seems to be going to hell
The inhabitants of this tranquil natural kingdom
Thankfully all still seem to be doing fairly well

An ancient oaken log soon entices me
So I wearily stretch out in the radiant sun
And my troubles soon begin to evaporate
My much needed rejuvenation has begun

The many songbirds living here all sing out so jubilantly
The squirrel rejoices in the gift of the glorious rising sun
The rabbit very gratefully eats his most nourishing meal
The newborn deer is thankful for the life it's just begun

The many trees lift their heads to the heavens in gratitude
The brightly colored butterflies joyously flitter all about
The many insects here happily sing their insect songs
All these living beings rejoicing in life without a doubt

After my long tranquil morning sojourn here is over
I am finally ready to face the grim world of man again
I rise and slowly begin walking home, fondly gazing back
Praying in my heart and soul that my sanctuary never ends

Spirits On The Wing

"The richness I achieve comes from Nature,
The source of my inspiration."

Claude Monet

Recently a cloud passed in front of the sun
It was a myriad of tiny winged spirits in flight
Looking very much like autumn leaves swirling
And filling those who spotted them with delight

They soon left our American borders
These tiny winged spirits in the wind
And they headed south for the winter
Not to return until spring again ushers in

They will winter down in Mexico
In the deep mountain forests of fir
Where they adore soaking up the sun
Their tiny bright colorful bodies all a stir

They begin arriving down in central Mexico
On *Dia de los Muertos* - The Day of the Dead
Some believe they are the spirits of dead children
And others the souls of departed warriors it is said

These wondrous marvels number in the millions
Their colors are tropical orange and midnight black
And I for one can't wait until I see these beings again
Anticipating the day these spirits on the wing will be back

Each Fall, tiny colorful Monarch butterflies vanish from Canada and the United States. They gather in Texas and all along the Gulf Coast, funneling into an invisible highway through the skies, instinctively heading south in gigantic waves to a place that their great-great-great grandparents left six months prior.

And for years, no one really knew where they went.

But after decades of searching for them, Cathy and Ken Brugger 'discovered' the Monarch winter colonies down in the pine and fir forests of Mexico on Jan. 2, 1975.

Scientists now believe that only here, in the boughs of fir trees at 10,000 feet, a four-hour drive west of Mexico City, can these butterflies find the 'delicate envelope' of climate they need to survive the long winter.

The local Mexican residents, of course, always knew about these Monarchs; they just didn't know where they summered, or that the rest of the world didn't know where they wintered.

Their journey north will begin again in late March, with Monarchs leaving the Mexican state of Michoacán, searching for milkweed as they fly, the only plant on which their caterpillars feed.

After they mate, the female Monarchs live only a few weeks. And it takes three or four generations of this wondrous creature to once again reach the Great Lakes, New England, and Canada.

In all the world, no butterflies migrate like the Monarchs of North America. They travel much farther than all other species, up to three thousand miles, and they are the only butterflies to make such a long, arduous, two way migration every year.

And amazingly, they instinctively fly en masse to the same winter roosts, often to the exact same trees, as their great-great-great grandparents did.

"In everything in Nature,
There is something of the marvelous."

Aristotle

North Shore Get-A-Way

"The happiest man,
Is he who learns from nature,
The lesson of worship."

Ralph Waldo Emerson

When life starts getting me down
I leave on a North Shore get-a-way
And in the fall, I know just the place
I head for Gooseberry Falls by the Bay

The autumn colors here start very early
The Falls have such a melodious sound
And despite a world now turned against it
Here I can still see glorious Nature abound

The North Shore is one of the very best places
To observe America's yearly Raptor migrations
Here, there are many types of truly wondrous birds
And my aching heart and soul soon soar with elation

Osprey, Bald Eagle, Northern Harrier, Cooper's Hawk
Golden Eagle, American Kestrel, and Northern Goshawk
And, of course, Common Loon, Wood Warbler, and Gull
On the merits of each one of these birds, I can always talk

Here I sit in sheer contentment and also watch other creatures
The Beaver, White-tailed Deer, Black Bear, and Screech Owl
And when I am extremely fortunate, and the forest gods allow
I peer up at the heavens, as I listen to a lone timber wolf howl

The Goose River first appeared on maps as far back as 1670
Named after either the French explorer *Sieur des Groseilliers*
Or an Ojibwa Native American word - *Shab-on-im-i-kan-i-sibi*
Both when translated, refer to the area's abundant gooseberries

Here in the ancient home of the Cree, the Dakotah, and the Ojibwa
I marvel at Nature's richness, and its many wildflowers and berries
Here, in a refuge, which I have always loved, on Lake Superior
I re-vitalize my heart and soul, and to leave, I'm never in a hurry

A Walk In Winter

"In seed time, learn;
In harvest, teach;
In winter, enjoy."

William Blake

I awoke before dawn
Feeling restless and blue
I knew that I needed a walk
For my waning spirit to renew

So very silently, I got dressed
And I headed off into the wood
A place my soul finds refreshment
A realm my mind and body feel good

As I traipsed down a secluded wooded path
I felt the crunch of fresh snow under my feet
Very often, when I'm feeling down and blue
I find myself seeking this most soothing retreat

Here, there are no modern distractions or war
Here, there is only God's wondrous Creation
Here, I still find the world as it was meant to be
Providing a very blissful, soul soothing, sensation

Soon, I inhaled the fragrant aroma of pine
What a marvelous, invigorating, natural smell
Before long, I sat down on an old oaken stump
And I silently listened for friends that here dwell

As I sat pondering, a wondrous serenade began
The tiny winged forest dwellers soon in full song
I closed my eyes, as they so cheerfully sang for me
And soon a feeling of serenity had righted my wrong

When I opened my eyes, I spotted a white-tailed deer
He was joyously listening to this free symphony, too
Sitting here all alone, amongst nature's splendid canvas
It usually doesn't take long for my waning spirit to renew

Before long, I felt several wet noses nuzzling my cheek
And now, I found my four very silent canines standing here
So now, the five of us pleasantly walked on through the snow
On this marvelous new winter's day, so fresh, bright, and clear

An Artist Came A Callin

"Every artist dips his brush in his own soul,
And paints his own nature into his pictures."

Henry Ward Beecher

An artist came to visit last night
While everyone here was sleeping
I thought I heard that crafty old rascal
At our windowpane very silently creeping

My vigilant dogs must have sensed him too
Because they acted awfully fidgety all night
And when I crawled out of bed this morning
My cats were admiring his work with delight

After I brewed my needed morning coffee
I sat in my kitchen window admiring it too
Old Jack truly knows how to paint a picture
He uses sparkling shades of silver and blue

Trees, bushes, and windows are his canvas
And his icy artistry is extremely meticulous
Old Jack's work is both stunning and serene
Nothing he ever paints ever looks ridiculous

And as I gazed out at his truly fine artistic work
I suddenly realized that he hadn't visited in awhile
I just kept gazing at it, and admiring his artistic style
But my dogs kept pestering, and I soon lost my smile

My four canines seemed to be in a real big hurry today
Their need to heed the call of nature was extremely plain
As we stepped out into a bone chilling blast of Arctic air
I realized that like many an artist, Jack Frost must be insane

The Ancient Apostle Islands

"Whenever the pressure of our complex city life
Thins my blood and numbs my brain,
I seek relief in the wilderness trail;
And when I hear the coyote wailing to the yellow dawn,
My cares fall from me - I am happy."

Hamlin Garland

There is a place that I like to go
To mark each long winter's end
And for as long as I possibly can
I will journey here again and again

Near the western edge of Lake Superior
Named by 17th Century Jesuit missionaries
These majestic islands called the Apostles
Always soon fill my heart and soul with glee

Containing numerous enchanting sea caves
And old lighthouses which guided many a ship
As each and every winter passes into a new spring
I always make visiting them an annual priority trip

Joyously wandering their serenely wooded natural trails
Pitching my old tent right down on the vast blue lakeshore
And soon reveling in all their magnificent beauty and wildlife
To herald Spring's arrival here is something that I truly do adore

These numerous island jewels of Lake Superior
Formed by ancient glacial ice, wind, and wave
Also contain many spectacular sandy beaches
And wondrous shoreline views that I truly crave

There is absolutely nothing more exhilarating
Than plunging into extremely chilly waves
The clean, clear, icy-cold Lake Superior water
Is truly life enhancing as it takes my breath away

Ojibwa Indians have many legends about these Apostles
Early French voyageurs once camped on these tiny lake isles
And while sitting around my brilliant red campfire each night
Picturing those historic long gone days always brings me a smile

And whenever there happens to be a brisk Lake Superior breeze
As I sit around my campfire with my dogs after darkness sets in
I can still hear the songs of these intrepid voyageurs and Ojibwas
Drifting through time and space, in these old Apostle Island winds

The Apostle Islands National Lakeshore was established in 1970 to conserve its magnificent natural splendor. And although named by early Jesuit Missionaries for the Twelve Apostles, there are actually 22 wondrous lake islands here.

And some of the Great Lakes' most spectacular scenery occurs on and around these tiny Lake Superior atolls where the forces of wave action, freezing, and subsequent thawing have interacted with the sandstone over the ages to create truly fascinating sea caves, delicate arches, vaulted chambers, and honeycombed passageways into numerous sandstone cliffs.

There are 35 species of mammals living within the boundaries of the Apostle Islands National Lakeshore, including black bear, wolf, deer, raccoon, skunk, coyote, fox, and red squirrel. And the Apostle Islands are truly a bird watcher's paradise. About 100 bird species breed on these islands, and over 240 different species have been identified within park boundaries.

And within the expansive stately forests of these Lake Superior shores, Nature lovers like myself bask under magnificent white pine, hemlock, yellow birch, cedar, sugar maple, red oak, birch, and balsam fir trees.

Hikers here also can enjoy more than fifty miles of maintained trails which provide access to historic old lighthouses, native artifacts, abandoned quarries, old farming sites, logging camps, beaches, and extremely scenic overlooks.

Camping opportunities on and around the Apostle Islands range from developed camp sites to primitive wilderness camping. And the Apostle Islands have long been a favorite Mecca for sailors and boaters. The islands' protected bays, public docks, pristine beaches, historic sites, and magnificent natural beauty offer outstanding boating and diving opportunities as well.

The Majestic, Historic, Lake Superior, Apostle Islands,
A Wondrous Place That I Always Enjoy Visiting Yet Again;
In Part II of This Poem The Wisdom Of Ojibwa Indian Lifestyle,
Ancient Native American Culture Always Inspires Me To No End

The Ancient Apostles – Part II

"We need to respect and learn from the things around us.
They teach us that everything struggles - deer, eagles, even the
smallest ant.
Just watch them for a while.
That's why we need to work together, and live with the world
around us,
Having respect for all these things, that are sacred."

An Ojibwa Elder

In days now long gone
They lived upon these islands
They respected earth's life forms
And the ties between animal and man

They were known as the native *Ojibwa* people
Their main village was called *Moningwunakauning*
It meant 'Home of the Yellow Breasted Woodpecker'
And much knowledge to their children they would bring

Offerings of food and tobacco were made to the Great Spirit
When the life of an animal was taken, everything on it was used
They had a genuine respect for the wisdom of their elder members
And nothing living on the lakes or in these forests was ever abused

From the great *Gitchee Gumee* they harvested fish
In the fall, they would harvest game and wild rice
In spring, they would tap the gigantic maple trees
The harvested sap was boiled so very tasty and nice

In the summer, they grew many plants and vegetables
They harvested succulent wild strawberries and blueberries
From the many white birch trees they built their sturdy canoes
A very simple life, but being in tune with nature, they were merry

They only took from nature what they needed
They knew that no human could own Earth's land
They were content to follow the Great Spirit's edicts
Until their simple lives were disrupted by the white man

Very callously and very cruelly, beginning in the mid to late 1800s
The government began confiscating their forest and island homes
Now, confined to small reservations, and stripped of hunting rights
Their way of life was gone, and to them, I now dedicate this poem

But as I wander among the ancient Apostle Islands even today
Especially when I perch gazing into the flames of my campfire
I can still both see and hear them, living so very contentedly here
And learning from their philosophy of life, is still my heart's desire

Thoughts of Hiawatha

"Forth upon the Gitche Gumee,
On the shining Big-Sea Water,
With his fishing line of cedar,
Of the twisted bark of cedar,
Forth to catch the Nahma,
Mishe-Nahma, King of Fishes,
In his birch canoe exulting,
All alone went Hiawatha."

Henry Wadsworth Longfellow,
From *The Song of Hiawatha*

'Dawn' what a magnificent word
What a truly wondrous time of day
As I rise and eagerly peer due east
The brilliant sun is already on display

It shines down on vast Lake Superior
Called *Gitche Gumee* by the old ones
It inspires and brings joyful new hope
That a truly brand new day has begun

It's time to forget yesterday's sorrows
Time to prepare for a brand new start
Time to again enjoy Nature's splendor
Time to rejuvenate my world weary heart

What will I do this glorious northwood morn?
As I dress and I peer across the *Gitche Gumee*
I decide like old Hiawatha, I will fish its bounty
A pastime that has always brought me much glee

As my boat engine slowly sputters to life
I begin cruising its magnificent shoreline
Now taking in all its splendid natural beauty
Yet one more chance given me by the Divine

The vast forest now fills with the joyous song of birds
The trees now all reverently bow in homage to the sun
A mother raccoon leads her babes to a life-giving drink
A glorious new northwood day has definitely now begun

Suddenly, a magnificent blue heron takes to wing
He silently glides above me in dawn's crisp new air
And a gigantic smallmouth bass rises from the depths
Ancient *Gitche Gumee's* magnificence is everywhere

As I peer off to the vast horizon towards the sun
I spot a lone figure in a canoe silently gliding by
When I look again, both man and canoe are gone
But they remain forever etched in my mind's eye

Although our fishing craft are somewhat different
At this moment I feel a true kinship with Hiawatha
As I take in all the sights and sounds of his paradise
My heart and soul now exult with happiness and awe

And very soon, I swear I can now somehow hear
An ardent whisper in the dawn's fresh new breeze,
*"Kitche-Manitou, The Great Creator Of All Things,
Please give me one more day, on the Gitche Gumee"*

Is this very soulful prayer from Hiawatha's Spirit?
Or somehow, from the subconscious essence, of Me?
But perhaps, it might be the fervent plea of this Bass,
So I place him back in *Gitche Gumee*, and set him Free

❀

The Great *Gitche Gumee* was also named *Le Lac Supérieur* in the seventeenth century by French explorers. It is the largest of North America's Great Lakes, the world's largest freshwater lake by surface area, and one of earth's very oldest.

On stormy days, waves as high as 31 feet have been recorded, and Lake Superior is the graveyard of more than 325 ships, also immortalized in Gordon Lightfoot's epic song, *The Wreck of the Edmund Fitzgerald.*

The *Gitche Gumee* stretches 380 miles east to west, and 160 miles across at its widest. It has an incredible 2,900 miles of shoreline, 31,820 square miles of surface area, an average depth of 489 feet, and an astounding maximum depth of 1,333 feet.

Its water clarity is also incredible, with visibility recorded to as much as 75 feet. Over the years, I've watched in true awe as many a great *Mishe-Nahma* has risen up from its mysterious depths, and I swear I've seen the ghost of old Hiawatha silently gliding by in his old birch bark canoe more than a few times, as well.

Thoughts of Hiawatha – II

"Ye who love the haunts of Nature,
Love the sunshine of the meadow,
Love the shadow of the forest,
Love the wind among the branches,
And the rain-shower and the snow-storm,
And the rushing of great rivers
Through their palisades of pine-trees,
And the thunder in the mountains,
Whose innumerable echoes
Flap like eagles in their eyres;
Listen to these wild traditions,
To this Song of Hiawatha."

Henry Wadsworth Longfellow

Whenever I find myself wandering the great northwood
I carry a tattered old copy of Longfellow's epic poem
A nun generously gave it to me back in grade school
And ever since, I've considered this forest my home

I believe Longfellow's words about Hiawatha's life
Inspired me to learn all I could about these woods
I know I would have loved living during his time
When our world seemed far more simple and good

Native peoples resided in their small communities
And they learned to respect and to love this land
They only took from it what they needed to survive
They knew that earth's natural resources were grand

They never killed any woodland creatures for 'sport'
They never chopped down entire live forests for greed
They never felt they were the only beings who mattered
Their innate harmony with Nature filled their every need

Somehow, when our world 'advanced' and became 'civilized'
We lost the respect and the admiration we once held for Creation
I still prefer to wander the woodlands, over visiting any large city
The forest is the only place my heart and soul still feels true elation

I think that I was sadly born a few centuries too late
I would have loved sitting around Hiawatha's campfire
Listening to him, and other very sage people of his day
Telling their ancient tales, with such passion and desire

Images of this forested paradise spoke deeply to Longfellow, who wrote *The Song of Hiawatha* as a tribute to Native American spirit and wisdom. His poem sold 10,000 copies in the first month it was published on November 10, 1855.

It centers on the life of an Ojibwa leader of the Great Lakes Region who loved his ancient northwood homeland immensely; and it speaks volumes to the green of this land, the blue of its water, the vibrant forest and its many magnificent furry and feathered children, a profound faith in God and Nature, Freedom, and a Deep Longing for Good.

And since my early childhood, *The Song of Hiawatha* has served me well:

"Through the leafy woods he wandered,
Saw the deer start from the thicket,
Saw the rabbit in his burrow,
Saw the pigeon, the 'Omeemee,'
Building nests among the pine trees."

And through these leafy woods,
I, too, will continue to wander,
For as long as the Creator allows.

Orange Sunrise

"Morning glory is the best name;
It always refreshes me to see it."

Henry David Thoreau

Whenever I have found myself traveling
To the wondrous expanses of the wilderness
I always eagerly arise before the crack of dawn
To watch a daily occurrence I don't want to miss

I anxiously get dressed in the darkness
Preparing for the first miracle of the day
Then I soon eagerly head off on horseback
To the nearest vantage point, without delay

Here I now sit in silent anticipation
Of yet another glorious new sunrise
Eagerly wondering what new visions
Will soon appear before my very eyes

And I don't remember ever being disappointed
As I perch extremely still silently facing due east
Because I know that I will very soon be rewarded
With an event that will be a most eye appealing feast

As the first new sunlight peeks over the vast horizon
The endless sky quickly takes on a brilliant orange hue
And the wildwood air is again fresh and clean and sweet
As the magnificent life cycle here once again begins anew

I have never found anything quite as soul soothing
As watching a brand new dawn atop a trusty equine
It's as if time has suddenly come to a complete halt
And this wondrous recurring event is all his and mine

This is also my favorite time of the day to give my humble thanks
For the natural splendor the Creator has placed here on this earth
And after joyously taking it all in, for a very lengthy leisurely time
We eagerly take off, starting another glorious day filled with mirth

And as we ride off through the uninhabited hills, lakes, and forests
Enjoying grand vistas and extremely panoramic views of the sky
Throughout the rest of our refreshing and peaceful day's sojourn
I always retain that image of another magnificent orange sunrise

End of Day

"Softly the evening came.
The sun from the western horizon,
Like a magician, extended his golden wand
O'er the landscape.
And sky and water and forest seemed all on fire,
And melted and mingled together."

Henry Wadsworth Longfellow

It had been another glorious day
Wandering the vast northland
And now it was time to watch
Yet another miracle most grand

If there's something more wondrous
Than a magical northwood sunset
Then I surely don't know about it
And I haven't discovered it yet

I stood in awe and admiration
Once again gazing due west
Another magnificent sunset
Perhaps one of the very best

I silently stood there taking it all in
On the edge of unblemished Creation
My heart and soul once again overjoyed
A feeling of total serenity now my sensation

Without any noisy distractions
Without any glaring city lights
Gazing at this heavenly wonder
Brought me such peaceful delight

And just before the light finally vanished
I heard my brother timber wolf call out to me
He told me that all was still all right in this place
As I listened to his howls echoing through the trees

And I know this is where I belong
For the remainder of my earthly days
I feel such a part of this land and water
A part of this landscape in so many ways

Over the years, I have traveled almost the entire world over
But I always seem to return here, to the splendid northwood
There is no other place I would rather spend my end of days
Than here, watching yet one more sunset, so wondrously good

Once Upon A Time

"In the United States today,
Each and every hour,
Of each and every day,
Over 36 acres of rural land,
Is being developed for:
Industrial, Residential,
And Recreational Use."

A Recent U.S. Government Report
On Urban Sprawl

Once upon a time
It was their world, too
Once upon a gentler time
Mankind was not as cruel

Today, we routinely invade their space
And we bulldoze right over their homes
Today, in this greedy modern world of ours
Most of them have almost nowhere left to go

Today, many of them now have to scavenge for food
In our giant garbage dumps, and in our homes' backyards
Today, many of them are callously run down on our roads
Today, for many of them, just staying alive is extremely hard

Today, in cities and towns all across America
Feral felines are rounded up and euthanized
Today, stray dogs are routinely shot on sight
And once, these abandoned pets were idolized

The once majestic, abundant, grizzly bear
Has now lost eighty percent of its home range
The once federally protected, noble, grey wolf
Is now being persecuted in the name of 'change'

Today, giant shopping malls and huge subdivisions
Are routinely being built in their swamps and wetlands
Making life extremely difficult for earth's migratory birds
Which at one time in our history, most of us found quite grand

Today, entire colonies of rabbits, gophers, and prairie dogs
Are buried alive as we construct yet one more factory parking lot
Today, municipalities fine people in parks for feeding pigeons
But for some, these winged birds are the only friends they've got

Today, cities and corporations now hire 'pest control' contractors
To murder every duck or goose, who dares to rest upon our ponds
Today, we have little compassion left for our nonhuman neighbors
Victims of our greed, with whom we have broken our ancient bond

Once upon a time,
It was their world, too;
Once upon a gentler time,
Mankind was not as cruel

Mourning The Manatee

"When all the beasts are gone,
Man will die from a great loneliness of spirit;
For whatever happens to the beasts,
Will also happen to the man."

Chief Seattle

In just the last five short years alone
Over sixteen hundred of them have died
They are tragically being killed by speedboats
Shoreline development and the dreaded Red Tide

This is an increase of eighteen percent
Over the prior five year period of time
Yet officials want to remove their protection
Taking them off the Endangered List – a true crime

It seems that boaters don't like speeding restrictions
And land developers don't like 'endangered death' fines
Unless we all take a stand in defense of our planet's animals
Many of them will soon be crossing the 'no return' extinction line

Faced with the largest number of manatee deaths in a decade, the
Florida Fish and Wildlife Conservation Commission (FFWCC) is
unbelievably planning to down-list the Manatee - a harmless,
gentle, sea creature known to body surf and barrel roll when
playing in shallow water - from *Endangered* to *Threatened.*

Just in the last five years, 1,682 of these gentle aquatic animals have died in Florida waters and of those; over 400 were killed by speedboats.   This is an almost 18 percent increase over the previous five-year period.

And marine biologists estimate that the dwindling Florida manatee population could drop by at least half in the next 50 years because of increased habitat loss, increased collisions with motor boats, and fatal Red Tide poisoning.

Red Tide is the name given to massive, harmful, oceanic and coastal river algae blooms that are increasingly occurring as a direct result of massive sewage, septic, fertilizer, and chemical runoff from our coastal cities, farms, and industries.

This Red Tide chokes off needed oxygen supplies in the water and creates devastating, life-robbing, oceanic 'Dead Zones.'

This latest extremely callous move against one of earth's numerous endangered animals is yet another 'triumphant' example of modern politics, modern human selfishness, and the ever increasing profit margins of modern day business concerns.

Manatees are now poised to be down-listed from the Endangered Species List by an agency supposedly tasked with protecting them, despite how poorly they are now faring in the wild because of a calculated effort by special interest groups opposed to both boating speed regulations and to any further restrictions on Florida shoreline development.

Manatees are extremely gentle, plant eating, marine mammals, sometimes nicknamed 'sea cows.'

They originated some 45 to 50 million years ago, and today, their closest living relatives on Earth are elephants.

And our coastal waters will truly be a much sadder place if these gentle giants soon disappear.

Mourning The Moose

"Every creature is better alive than dead,
Men and moose and pine trees;
And he who understands this,
Would rather preserve life, than destroy it. "

Henry David Thoreau

Sadness now fills my heart
As I read a wildlife magazine
Another wondrous forest creature
May soon be disappearing it seems

The magnificent northwood moose
Its numbers are declining drastically
It needs extremely frigid temperatures
Yet another global warming catastrophe

It seems that tiny deer parasites are the cause
The warmer temperatures allow them to thrive
As I sit in my living room pondering this report
I sadly wonder how long the moose will survive

I also sit here recalling many wondrous encounters
With these creatures of the northwood on many a day
I have observed them swimming in magnificent blue lakes
I've watched them feeding, nurturing their young, and at play

I truly cannot imagine the glorious forests of the great northwood
Depleted of yet another of North America's magnificent creatures
Sadness encompasses my heart and my soul, pondering all of this
Destruction of earth and nature–truly mankind's very worst feature

Often tipping the scales at nearly 1,000 pounds and standing 6-feet tall, moose are iconic in my beloved northwood, and glimpsing one of them still thrills many a northwood resident and tourist alike. They have thrilled me since my early childhood days.

"They are the true symbol of the wilderness. You see it all throughout the North Country, in the names of towns, rivers, cafes—everything under the sun," says a Minnesota Department of Natural Resources wildlife researcher, who is now studying this very tragic moose decline.

This latest scientific study has concluded that climate change, combined with these deer parasites and severe malnutrition, have caused the moose population to plunge.

If temperatures continue to rise, these magnificent creatures could disappear from North America forever in the next 50 years.

"The moose are now gone,
And their bones lie under the sand in the soft coal,
Which was once the forest, by the estuary..."

Henry Williamson

Red Knot Requiem

"There is nothing in which birds differ more from man
Than the way in which they can build,
And yet leave a landscape as it was before."

Robert Lynd

They are true masters of long distance aviation
They wing their way almost 20,000 miles a year
They are one of earth's most remarkable creatures
And for these unique birds we should all shed a tear

On their annual migrations between South America
And their summering grounds in the Arctic northland
They must stop to rest and to eat horseshoe crab eggs
In Delaware Bay, located off New Jersey's coastland

But the once plentiful horseshoe crab is woefully in decline
Because of massive over fishing it may never come back again
And many marine biologists on the eastern seaboard now believe
That the once abundant Red Knot may be extinct as early as 2010

Yet another nonhuman earth resident,
That is truly in dire jeopardy today;
And I sadly wonder how many more,
For our modern human greed – will pay

The Red Knot is the largest of the sandpipers in North America, and one of the most colorful. And it makes one of the longest yearly migrations of any bird, traveling from its Arctic breeding grounds to Tierra del Fuego in southern South America.

These Red Knots concentrate in huge numbers at traditional staging grounds during their annual migrations, and Delaware Bay is an important area for them since these birds have fed on the eggs of spawning horseshoe crabs here for countless centuries.

It's estimated that nearly 90 percent of the entire Red Knot population can be present on the bay in a single day, and the drastic reduction in food available to these birds here because of modern day over harvesting of horseshoe crabs is responsible for a drastic decline in Red Knot populations today.

These birds "have gone from an undeniably majestic display of nature to a tragic remnant," says the head of the New Jersey Department of Environmental Protection's Endangered and Nongame Species Program.

Once, over 100,000 Red Knots flocked to Delaware Bay each spring; last year the count was only about 13,000.

If this magnificent winged creature soon does become extinct, the Red Knot will very sadly join the Carrier Pigeon and 10 other U.S. bird species that have already tragically vanished from the face of the Earth since John James Audubon first painted North America's majestic birds in the 1800s.

Where's The Buzz?

"Teaching a child not to step on a caterpillar,
Is as valuable to the child as it is to the caterpillar."

Bradley Millar

I have been interested in all types of insects
Since my early childhood days in our backyard
My grandmother taught me how important they are
And even for bugs, life on earth has now become hard

One of our most important insects, the honey bee
Is mysteriously vanishing from these United States
Honey bees pollinate every third bite of food we eat
Without them, our crops face a most horrendous fate

Ninety of our cultivated flowering food crops
From red apples to watermelons and cranberries
Rely almost exclusively on honey bee pollination
And without it, our lives will become far less merry

Since at least the 1980s, many scientists and biologists
Have been urging increased usage of other tiny pollinators
But of course, like so many other warnings we've neglected
Most folks just shrugged and said, 'We'll worry about it later'

Well sadly, 'later' has suddenly become 'right now'
Other natural pollinators, like the butterfly and wasp
Are also not doing very well in our heavily polluted land
If bees don't make a comeback, our food sources could stop

As we now rely on the Middle East for most of our crude oil
One day very soon, we could face a massive import of our food
And as we have seen from the poisoned pet food and tainted toys
Facing a future relying on imports should truly dampen our mood

❀

Scientists are calling this massive honey bee die-off 'Colony Collapse Disorder' (CCD). First reported in Florida, the problem has already spread to 24 states, and commercial beekeepers are now reporting losses of between 50 and 90 percent of their hives all across the country.

While food crops like wheat and corn are pollinated by the wind, some 90 of our cultivated flowering crops rely heavily on the honey bee for pollination.

"Honey bees pollinate every third bite of food ingested by we Americans," reports a Cornell University study, and honey bees help generate some $14 billion in American produce.

Research is only now beginning on our vanishing honey bees, and hard data is still woefully lacking, but beekeepers suspect everything from a new modern day virus or parasite to toxic pesticides and genetically modified crops.

Scientists have now hastily established a CCD working group, and for many American farmers, this current honey bee crisis is a terrible wake-up call.
By relying on a single species of insect for pollination for so long now, U.S. agriculture has put itself in a very precarious position. A resilient agricultural system requires diverse pollinators, and scientific evidence also indicates a vast decline in our other

potential alternate food pollinators – native species of butterflies, wasps, and other types of bees.

Many now believe that the blame for our disappearing honey bees sits squarely on our modern day human activities – severe habitat loss, widespread pesticide usage, air and land pollution, and imported insect predators and disease.

And, unbelievably, we're still using some very deadly pesticides on our American crops that were banned in many European countries years ago.

Once, There Were Millions

"In 1870, one could travel for mile upon mile,
Without seeing so much as a traveler's bivouac.

Millions of buffalo darkened the rolling plains.
There were deer, elk, and wolves on every hill,
And in every ravine and thicket.

By the autumn of 1883,
There was not a buffalo remaining on the range,
And the deer, elk, and wolves were already scarce."

Granville Stuart,
Nature and History In The American West

For countless centuries
These wild bison had thrived
But within a few short years
There were barely any left alive

It's estimated they once numbered
In the thirty to fifty million range
Today, less than 1 percent survive
About 4,000 still cling to life today

In 1872, Congress had very wisely established
Yellowstone National Park, to give them refuge
And now, even here, in the very last home they have
They are once again under attack, and are about to lose

Modern day cattle ranching corporations want them gone
They claim bison carry disease and eat far too much grass
Yet, these cattle ranchers receive huge government subsidies
To graze their cattle on public land on which their cattle get fat

Just this past winter, over 1,000 bison were captured and killed
Because cattle ranchers have clout and contribute to our politicians
Hearings are being held in Congress to decide the fate of the bison
Will we stand up to save them, or lead a new species to extinction?

Not All That Very Long Ago,
There Were Millons and Millions of Them;
And Soon, These Wild Bison May Be Gone, Forever,
How Many More Species, Will Our Human Greed End?

Wild Horses

"Wild free-roaming horses
Are living symbols
Of the historic and pioneer spirit of the American West,
And, therefore, they must be protected."

A Congressional Declaration - Dec. 15, 1971

A little over one hundred very short years ago
Two million wild horses roamed the American West
Artist George Catlin captured their magnificent spirit
In one of his paintings – which I think is one of his best

Then, with the arrival of the 1900s
Their horrendous slaughter soon began
Thousands of them were butchered for market
By the unstoppable insatiable greed of Modern Man

At the request of very many outraged United States citizens
In 1971, Congress finally passed legislation to protect them
Most people in the 1970s still revered our national treasures
Most people didn't want the freedom of these mustangs to end

But very unbelievably, back on January 25, 2005,
Congress acted to restore their horrendous slaughter and sale
Bowing to cattlemen and overseas horseflesh market demand
On wild horse coffins, they were greedily pounding the final nail

Today there are less than 30,000 wild horses in the U.S.
And our government plans to reduce them even further

Selling off their flesh to food markets in Europe and Asia
Yet one more American treasure - - to be savagely murdered

America's wild horses and burros had been protected from slaughter from 1971-2005, but in 2004, former U.S. Senator Conrad Burns (R-Montana) stripped those protections by craftily slipping an amendment into the 2005 omnibus spending bill.

And that's when their horrendous slaughter began again. Thousands of our wild horses have since been slaughtered in three foreign owned slaughter houses on U.S. soil, and thousands more have been carted off to Mexico and to Canada for slaughter.

After thousands of phone calls, e-mails, and letters, America's horse and animal welfare advocates recently won two victories in Congress, both key steps toward a permanent ban on horse slaughter for human consumption overseas.

Based on considerable public pressure, the U.S. House of Representatives recently passed a bill reinstating protections of wild free-roaming horses and burros from commercial sale and slaughter. This bill, H.R. 249, passed with overwhelming support by a vote of 277 to 137.

This House vote came a day after the Senate Commerce Committee passed a similar bill, S. 311, The American Horse Slaughter Prevention Act; legislation that would permanently ban horse slaughter for human consumption in the United States, and would ensure that our horses could not be shipped to other countries for the same purpose.

The continued survival of our magnificent wild horses in the United States is already threatened by the recent loss of 13 million acres of land originally granted to manage this species, and now given over by our elected officials to corporate cattle ranchers.

Cries In The Night

"Man is not Man,
But a Ravenous Wolf,
To Those He Does Not Know."

Titus Maccius Plautus

I can hear his sad lament
In the ever decreasing wild
I can hear his cries of anguish
In my dreams every once in awhile

The noble ancient ancestor of the dog
Is once again under attack by mankind
He is now hunted down by air in Alaska
In our national parks, no solace can he find

New plans are underway to award 'Kill Bounties'
For those that murder his kind in Yellowstone Park
Every day there are fewer places for him to now hide
As he and his family are forced to scavenge in the dark

And oh, the atrocious lies mankind tells about him
Even though this ancient creature never attacks man
The wolf was given the task of keeping Balance in Nature
But modern mankind so arrogantly ignores the Creator's Plan

This year, I decided to donate to 'The Toys For Tots' Program
By giving a Plush Wolf Toy and a Wolf Certificate of Adoption
I pray the needy child who receives it grows to be a nature lover
And becomes part of a caring generation that ends his destruction

I can hear his sad lament,
In the ever decreasing wild;
I can hear his cries of anguish,
In my dreams every once in awhile

And if you would also now like to learn
How to help both endangered animals and Earth's needy tots
Please visit an animal advocate website like *World Wildlife Fund*
Many of our earthly neighbors need all the compassion we've got

Mother Ocean's Sorrow

"This is probably the center,
Where many of the species evolved,
And spread to other parts of the ocean,
So it's going back to the source in many ways."

Dr. Larry Madin,
Deep Sea Project Leader

We've destroyed so much on Mother Earth
And most of it, all within the last 200 years
Far too many land life forms are already extinct
And for that, each of us should be shedding tears

Man now longs to explore deep space
And we're fascinated by oceans' deep
A new team of explorers is now diving
Into the vast depths of the Celebes Sea

It was formed they say, over 42 million years ago
Part of the western Pacific, out near the Philippines
It is a very ancient ocean basin, as deep as 16,000 feet
With mysterious unknown life forms we have never seen

A team of scientists from the U.S. and the Philippines
Is now studying this area of the ocean more extensively
Collecting marine samples, possibly millions of years old
And searching for clues to the earliest forms of life in the sea

As we kill off and destroy more and more life forms on land
There are many forms of sea life, we have not even identified
But as Modern Man now pollutes earth's many oceans, as well
I wonder how many unknown life forms may have already died

Science tells us life on earth once began in our mysterious oceans
And without interference, life's existed there for millions of years
I pray our quest for knowledge, doesn't lead to more destruction
And I sadly wonder if many unknown life forms, now live in fear

Big City Sunday Morning

"To find the universal elements enough;
To find the air and the water exhilarating;
To be refreshed by a morning walk or an evening saunter;
To be thrilled by the stars at night;
To be elated over a bird's nest or a wildflower in spring –
These are some of the true rewards of life."

John Burroughs

An extremely lovely early Sunday morning
A leisurely stroll along the big city's skyline
While most folks had not yet gotten out of bed
We were already enjoying an experience divine

The sky was a vivid heavenly blue
Boats at anchor in the warm breeze
As we sauntered along hand in hand
Many marvelous wonders for us to see

The bright new sun peeking over the horizon
Seagulls beginning to soar in the new day's air
Although we were exploring in a city of millions
Nature's wondrous gifts surrounded us everywhere

Eventually, we came upon a very important new artistic exhibit
Below it, a most profound message we both took the time to read
My wife, a life-long educator, and myself, an avowed nature lover
Both of us hoping the inscribed words many will now finally heed:

'Raise Future Environmentalists'

Teach your children well.

Go outside with them,
And discover a robin's egg,
A wild rose, or a waterfall.

Until our kids love and connect with nature
On a personal level, they won't be motivated to protect it.

Where will future environmentalists come from,
If video games and big screen TVs
Leave no time for climbing trees and catching fireflies?

When parents encourage outdoor exploration
And respect for nature,
Kids learn the value of protecting our planet.

Instead of just reading about faraway rainforests and
endangered species,
Go out together, and experience nature's wonders firsthand.

Skip rocks on a lake, and picnic in the park.
Go camping.
Hike in the Grand Canyon, or walk in the local forest preserve.

Help children feel comfortable in the natural world,
Before you ask them to heal it.

When was the last time you explored nature with your child?

Nancy Pochis Bank, 'Nature Nurture'

❋

As my spouse and I eventually trekked off together
We knew that this artistic message was deeply profound
Earth's future truly lies in the hands of children living today
A new generation of environmentalists must quickly be found

Most politicians today don't care about the environment
Our dedicated teachers can only do so much in our schools
If we, ourselves, don't start teaching children to respect nature
They'll soon inherit a bleak artificial world, in which apathy rules

What Will You Be Doing,
With Your Kids and Grandkids This Weekend?

"We Will Be Known Forever,
By The Tracks We Leave."

A Native American Proverb

Ode To An Environmentalist

"The more clearly we can focus our attention
On the wonders and realities of nature,
The less taste we shall have for its destruction."

Rachel Carson

May 27, 2007, marked the 100th Anniversary of Rachel Louise Carson's birth. She's always been one of my heroes. She was a marine biologist, taught Zoology at the University of Maryland, worked for the U.S. Fish and Wildlife Service, is largely responsible for the creation of The Environmental Protection Agency and The Endangered Species Act, and she wrote *Silent Spring*.

This was a book that generated tons of controversy when it was first published in 1962. The extremely powerful U.S. pesticide industry tried very hard to have this book suppressed, and it immediately challenged her findings concerning the widespread usage of toxic pesticides, including DDT.

Carson was vehemently attacked by the chemical industry and many in our own government as an alarmist, but she courageously spoke out to remind us that we humans are a vulnerable part of the natural world, subject to the same damage as the rest of Earth's ecosystem.

When CBS Television scheduled an hour-long news report on Carson's condemnation of the 'rivers of death' the chemical industry were pouring into our country's fresh water supply, two corporate television sponsors immediately withdrew their support. But the proverbial cat was now out of the bag, and her book remained on the Bestseller List for months; and, it remains in print now, 46 years later.

Testifying before Congress in 1963, Carson called for new policies to protect human health and the environment. Rachel Carson died in 1964, after a long battle with breast cancer. But her witness for the beauty and integrity of life continues to inspire many of us to protect the living world, and all its living creatures.

In fact, Rachel Carson's epic book helped millions of us to finally develop an 'environmental consciousness,' and that was no small accomplishment. Among other noteworthy elements of her book, it introduced the term 'Ecosystem' to the general public.

Rachel Louise Carson, a true American Hero, finally made 'Environmentalism' respectable.

Before the publication of *Silent Spring*, nearly all Americans believed that science was always 'a force for good.' Carson's work truly exposed the dark side of science and modern technology, and it conclusively showed that DDT and other toxic chemicals we were using to enhance agricultural productivity were truly poisoning our lakes, rivers, oceans, animals, and even ourselves.

Thanks to her, progress can no longer be measured solely in tons of wheat produced and millions of insects killed.

Thanks to her, the massive modern day destruction of Nature can no longer be called 'Progress.'

In 1992, a panel of distinguished Americans declared Rachel Carson's *Silent Spring* the most influential book of the past 50 years.

And this was one of the latest in a long line of tributes to a woman who almost single-handedly alerted Americans to the dark side of science in alliance with powerful business interests. Her measured, carefully-worded, yet passionate prose was all the more damning because she, herself, was a noted scientist.

Rachel Carson died in 1964 at the young age of 57, but her legacy will live on forever.

She was posthumously awarded the Presidential Medal of Freedom, and thanks to her, magnificent animals like the Osprey featured in my poem, *Lady of the Lake*, have been given a new lease on life. But our environmental work, has sadly just begun:

"We stand now, where two roads diverge.
But unlike the roads in Robert Frost's familiar poem,
They are not equally fair.

The road we have long been traveling is deceptively easy,
A smooth superhighway on which we progress with great speed,
But at its end lies disaster.

The other fork of the road / the one less traveled,
Offers our last, our only chance, to reach a destination
That assures the preservation of Earth."

Rachel Carson

America's National Park System

"Within our national parks,
There will be room,
Glorious room,
For both our wild animals,
And for all of us,
To find ourselves, to think, and to hope,
To dream and to plan, to rest, and to resolve."

Enos A. Mills,
The Father of Rocky Mountain National Park

I have visited Rocky Mountain National Park, and many of the other glorious national parks in the United States over the past 50 years, and I for one, have always loved them. And I for one have always been extremely grateful that concerned citizens and our government had both the foresight and the initiative to preserve some of our rapidly diminishing wilderness areas for future generations of Americans to enjoy.

The scenery in these national parks has always been breath-taking; the air and landscape quite pristine; and the joy and serenity to be found in them has always been beyond compare.

And the numerous wild animals that inhabit our national park system have continued to capture both the curiosity and the hearts of Americans over the years. The opportunity to observe many of these magnificent animals in a very natural setting has been a major drawing card for our national parks such as Rocky

Mountain, Glacier, Yellowstone, Yosemite, the Everglades, and many more.

America's national parks have always provided some of the best, and sadly, some of the very last remaining habitats for countless North American animal species. In fact, over one-third of the endangered and threatened species in our nation today can be found within our national park boundaries.

But very sadly to me, and to many other nature lovers, our national park system today is now headed for ruin. And we, the American people, are letting it happen right under our noses.

What kind of modern legacy will we be leaving to our children, and to our grandchildren? And what will future generations of soon to be deprived Americans think of us for allowing it to happen so easily?

Today, most of our national parks are increasingly being damaged, parceled off, and pilfered by endless urban development, by air and water pollution, by far too much uncontrolled recreational usage, and even worse, by very callous and very greedy modern day business concerns.

Today, both our national parks and our remaining American wildlife are in great jeopardy.

To me, and to many others, these national parks and their magnificent flora and fauna are among America's greatest remaining treasures; yet we are indifferently sitting by as our politicians and our corporations decimate them, instead of helping us to protect and to preserve them as intended by our forefathers.

'The Roadless Rule,' once very sacred in our national park system, has now been quickly swept away to make it much easier for modern day business concerns, logging interests, and mining companies to pursue their gluttonous business interests, and their huge profits.

On an ever increasing basis, all-terrain vehicles, snowmobiles, and motorbikes are now tearing up delicate ecosystems and natural habitat in our once pristine national parks.

More and more of our endangered wildlife are being targeted for slaughter by modern day commercial interests inside national park boundaries, and directly adjacent to them.

Our once treasured historic national park lodges and rustic old inns are now rapidly being sold off and torn down by both foreign and domestic business concerns, many of them now regarding our once treasured national park wildlife as 'nuisances,' or as 'easy meal tickets' for hungry overseas meat and fur markets.

Business lobbyists, our legislators, and even our President, are increasingly calling for more and more commercialization and destruction of our remaining national park system.

Our government is already allowing corporations to sponsor corporate events on our national park land; to post gaudy advertisements for their modern products on our hiking trails and ski areas; and new Forest Service rules even override any state laws prohibiting advertisements for tobacco, liquor, and gambling on federal land.

Many of us already have extremely horrifying visions of our once pristine national parks soon becoming just another modern day blight on the land – filled with junky corporate billboards, garish strip malls, gigantic subdivisions, resort hotels, casinos, golf courses, even more abysmal junk food restaurant chains, and worst of all, toxic waste dumps.

A gigantic modern day cell phone tower already hideously looms almost directly over Old Faithful. Reports indicate that the National Park Service no longer even knows how many of these gigantic cell phone towers now loom over our national park system because many of these modern day business deals are conveniently made in private - out of public scrutiny.

Our National Park Rangers are also probably the most revered of all our government employees – and deservedly so. Yet, even they are in danger of losing more and more of their jobs since many of our leaders now propose 'out-sourcing' more and more of these once extremely needed government jobs to private, modern day, contractors.

A recent White House Privatization Plan called for the transfer of more than one half of our National Park jobs - including rangers, firefighters, archaeologists, and biologists - to private business contractors.

And I for one, doubt very seriously that these private contractors will love our national park system, and its many wild creatures, as much as these extremely dedicated public servants do, and have always done.

But even sadder to me, and to many others, is what private business concerns and powerful sporting interests have in store for, and are already doing to, our once revered national park wildlife, magnificent scenery, and delicate ecosystems.

Bison

Since last January, the National Park Service has allowed the killing of more than 1,000 Yellowstone Park wild bison (American Buffalo). These animals are national symbols, yet in late 2005, Montana opened its first buffalo hunt in 15 years, and hundreds of them were slaughtered before the end of the year. Modern day business lobbyists claim they eat too much grass.

Bears

The Katmai bear population is one of the most photographed wildlife species remaining in the world today. Thousands of visitors flock to Alaska each year to catch a glimpse of these magnificent creatures in their natural habitat.

Yet the Alaska Board of Game is now allowing brown bears to be hunted beyond what is sustainable in Katmai National Preserve-- and they are set to open up 95,000 additional acres of land right inside Katmai National Park to bear hunting for the first time in decades.

Wild Horses

These wild mustangs have freely roamed the American West for centuries, and today, even on our once protected national park land, they are being slaughtered at an ever increasing rate. Why? To feed a ravenous overseas human market for horseflesh, and to appease modern day cattle ranchers.

These huge modern day cattle ranchers lease our national park land at a fraction of the cost to graze their cattle on privately owned land, yet they be-grudge the wild stallion's continued presence on it, and that of the American Bison – on our public land – and our own government is allowing them to do so. But so are we all.

Wolves

Our government sought to completely wipe out wolves in most of America's national parks beginning in the 19th century, and by 1926, they had successfully done so.

But beginning in the 1940s, as more and more biologists slowly came to understand the extremely important and very necessary role of predators in any natural ecosystem, a strong constituency was built up in favor of restoring wolves to national park areas where they had been extirpated. Thus, the Wolf was once again protected, and it was soon added to the ever increasing North American Endangered Animal Species List.

But despite this federal protection and the current public sentiment in favor of our wolves, these once nearly extinct wild animals are once again in modern day crosshairs.

At least 21 reintroduced Mexican wolves have been illegally shot in New Mexico and Arizona on or near public land.

There are dozens of unsolved grey wolf killings in the state of Idaho, where they have also been reintroduced by the government; and, unbelievably, Alaskan wildlife officials have now resumed aerial gunning of wolves to maximize their moose and caribou herds for out of state hunters with lots of cash.

Elk hunting is also a multi-million-dollar sporting event on the public lands that surround Yellowstone National Park, and today, sport hunters seem to be a very powerful political constituency as well. Many of these elk hunters now blame wolves for decimating Yellowstone's current elk population, and efforts are once again underway to eradicate them. But wolves are just one small factor in our ever increasing elk population decline.

As wolves were being reintroduced to these national park areas, wildlife officials also increased elk-hunt quotas to appease these hunters, and a very prolonged drought, probably caused by Global Warming, is quickly reducing their once abundant forage, diminishing our elk numbers even more.

Many members of the cattle and sheep ranching community, another very powerful modern day interest group, also claim that these wolves are now threatening their modern day livelihood. A century ago, livestock predation was a serious concern in America. Today, however, wolves account for only a tiny fraction of livestock deaths.

Of the 104 million head of cattle raised in the United States in 2005, wolves killed only 4,400 of them, according to U.S. Department of Agriculture statistics. By contrast, severe digestive problems caused 648,000 livestock deaths in 2005.

And we are the ones eating the vast majority of these cattle, not the wolves.

Moreover, ranchers who lose any livestock to wolves today are compensated for their losses by the government; yet, they too, no longer wish to share our nation with the once again beleaguered wolf.

Glacier National Park

Glacier National Park, which sits on the Canadian border, is one of my favorite national parks; I've visited there many times; and its scenery is quite spectacular. Yet, it could very soon be turned into an abysmal Modern Day Waste Dump.

That's the hideous sight that might soon greet Glacier Park visitors if a huge modern mining corporation gets its way – and they probably will. This corporation is proposing a massive open-pit coal mine operation in the headwaters of the Flathead River, which forms Glacier Park's western boundary.

This massive open-pit mine would sit directly within the spectacular views of Glacier National Park, and it would include several massive waste dumps on the river. The Flathead River supports a wide array of wildlife, including wolves, lynx, moose, and the extremely endangered grizzly bear. Furthermore, the contaminated mine runoff would threaten the already jeopardized trout population in this once very pristine river system.

✻

This is just a tiny glimpse of the extremely grim future of America's National Park System, and the very grim future of its once protected and revered wild animals. There are many more horrifying stories today, and some of them are occurring at a national park very near your own home.

What's happened to our very sage American idea of serene, natural, federally protected wilderness areas that all Americans could enjoy – for countless American generations to come?

What's happened to all of us, and to our modern day value system? And to our once great concern for future generations of our fellow citizens, and the future of wildlife not yet born on this continent?

In just eight short years, America will celebrate the 100th Anniversary of our National Park System. But now, I have to wonder if many of our once revered national parks will even exist anymore in the year 2016 - in the way they were once envisioned to continue to exist, in perpetuity, and in harmony with nature, by Enos Mills and many other dedicated American conservationists.

"National Parks
Will be our islands of safety in this riotous world.
Splendid forests, the waterfalls that leap in glory,
The wild flowers that charm and illuminate the earth,
The wild sheep of the sky-line crags, and the beauty of the birds;
All will have places of refuge, right here, in our national parks."

Enos A. Mills,
1915

I sadly wonder what wise old Enos would think about the sad plight of our national parks today.

If we care at all about America's National Park System, and what's very hideously happening to it today, it's about high time we all do something about it – before it's much too late.

I Cry

I cry for the ever-vanishing countryside I enjoyed so much in my youth. I cry for America's abandoned pets. I cry for the thousands of innocent wild creatures we displace and destroy each and every day in our never- ending lust for urban expansion.

I cry for our mistakes, and for our greed, and for our stupidity. I cry, because we have somehow lost our way.

As a child, my love of nature, animals, and the great outdoors increased with each and every passing year – in the very heart of one of America's biggest cities. And if I wanted to see more of nature's splendor, all I had to do was hop on a commuter train or bus and ride it to the city limits.

There, I would scamper off and immediately stand in awe of gigantic green forests filled with frolicking wild creatures, peaceful meadows, and serene rivers, ponds, and creeks. Beyond the forest, as far as my eyes could see, small family farms, rustic fruit stands, livery stables, natural prairies, and wondrous wetlands dotted the landscape. And, they all flourished.

I rode horses, went exploring in the vast prairies and wetlands, watched the dairy cows grazing in the lush green fields, bought delicious, freshly ripened fruit, and fished to my heart's content – all right outside the city limits of one of America's largest cities.

Today, as I journey here and there to favorite childhood haunts– my heart breaks. I cannot believe my eyes. I cannot believe what has happened to my homeland. I cannot believe our stupidity, or our greed.

The once proud family wheat farm is now a huge corporate subdivision with a thousand prefabricated houses that all look exactly alike.

The rustic old horse ranch is now an abysmal strip mall, overflowing with junky shops and tasteless fast food chains.
The good old fishing hole has been filled in and paved over to make way for a super king-sized corporate department, grocery, and quick change motor oil store.

The quaint old pumpkin patch is now covered over in concrete. It has now sadly been transformed into a bustling, 24-hour, drive-thru, corporate pharmacy and mini-mart, specifically designed for the extremely busy modern person who is too busy to even get out of his/her car.

Not that long ago, the great green areas surrounding our big cities were teeming with fascinating nonhuman creatures such as white-tailed deer, opossums, raccoons, rabbits, skunks, woodchucks, beavers, barn owls, hawks, ducks, geese, foxes, and coyotes.

We had our cities; they had their countryside. It was an extremely nice balance of nature, and we usually left each other alone.

When I was a child traveling on the highways and byways surrounding our big cities, I often counted cows, horses, and wild creatures to pass the time. Children riding in areas encircling our big cities today often count animal 'road kill.'

Thousands of feral felines are now routinely rounded up and summarily destroyed in cities, suburbs, government facilities, and military installations all across this vast nation.

And very sadly, the majority of these innocent creatures are the woefully neglected and rejected offspring of someone's discarded, unwanted, and un-neutered pet.

Thousands of affectionate, frightened, abandoned canines languish in city pounds and animal shelters all across America today, while atrocious puppy mills continue to mass-produce pedigreed dogs to sell to the wholesale dog industry, which includes both pet stores and research facilities. Many of these puppy mills house both their 'breeder bitches' and their highly priced offspring in squalid, cramped conditions, often in their own feces.

And sadly, many of these dogs will also end up in animal pounds and shelters after they outlive their show, hunt, and research usefulness.

Thousands of young Rottweiler, Doberman, and Bull Terrier pups are viciously beaten, tortured, and starved by their savage human owners who want them to guard their illicit guns and drugs or train them to participate in mortal combats for cash. These innocent creatures are not born vicious; vicious human beings make them so.

The reputation of these canine breeds is so horrendous today that many municipalities now want to ban them as pets; many animal shelters refuse to adopt them out; many insurance companies refuse to insure their owners; and many police officers, in true fear for their lives, shoot them on sight.

If our once beloved pets are now being so callously abandoned, abused, tortured, vilified, and killed in America today, what chance will our wild animal neighbors have? I wonder.

A terrified starving coyote was recently found cowering under the wheels of a taxicab in the very heart of downtown Chicago. Numerous suburban municipalities now hold sanctioned deer kills to rid themselves of these extremely peaceful woodland creatures that were once considered majestic; and are now deemed to be pests.

Bird lovers across America are now routinely fined for feeding pigeons in the park.   Many cities, towns, and suburban subdivisions across this land are also now banning birdfeeders.

An alligator recently wandered into a suburban Texas subdivision built on swampland, this wild creature's natural habitat.   It was savagely tied by its neck to the back of a pickup truck, dragged through the suburban streets in front of dozens of resident children, and eventually shot dead.   When captured, this alligator had not approached, threatened, or harmed anyone.

Waterfowl, by nature, are attracted to water.   Yet, when artificial, aesthetically pleasing ponds and drainage ditches are constructed at suburban office complexes and subdivisions all across this vast country today, hundreds of complaints are soon registered concerning the inevitable arrival of messy, noisy, ducks and geese. Numerous corporations hire modern day contractors to destroy the eggs or disrupt the nests of these innocent wild creatures.

In a hilly suburban area in Colorado, an entire colony of prairie dogs was recently destroyed as their homes were flattened and paved over for a new parking lot. Dozens of burrows were scraped flat, crushing to death or burying alive the numerous animals trapped below.   Numerous human volunteers had been willing to live-trap and relocate these harmless creatures.   Their humane efforts were declined.

If we are no longer even willing to share our suburban land and water with our earthly nonhuman neighbors, perhaps we should no longer build suburbs in swamps, wetlands, and forests, or construct wildlife attracting suburban ponds. Perhaps we should stop callously invading and destroying their natural habitats in the first place.

Does anyone in our ever-expanding urban American environment today even remember that these nonhuman neighbors of ours were here first? Does anyone even care anymore?

Are these really the new legacies and traditions that we wish to pass down to our future offspring regarding the status of animals on this planet? I sincerely hope not.

Must we humans be so arrogant? Must we humans be so gluttonous? Must we humans be so blind? Must we destroy every blade of prairie grass, every isolated wetland, every stand of white pine, every clump of naturally occurring dirt, and every chipmunk, sparrow, and spider that stands in the way of 'progress?' I sincerely hope not.

Must the docile deer soon walk the path of the now butchered buffalo? For the sake of future generations of both animals and kindred Nature lovers, I sincerely hope not.

Today, on a daily basis, we callously chase off, dig out, bury, poison, snare, shoot, maim, and run over our nonhuman neighbors. We bulldoze, uproot, scatter, and kill thousands of them each and every day. Our gluttonous penchant for urban sprawl has left these innocent victims with little or no refuge. They are simply in the way of our never-ending thirst and lust to expand our already gigantic, concrete, artificial world.

Sadly, the future appears very bleak. Sprawling land development is gobbling up the American countryside at an alarming rate of 36.5 acres per hour according to U.S. Government statistics.

Soon, our nonhuman earthly neighbors will have nowhere left to run. Someday soon, our future offspring may have to visit a zoo just to see what a raccoon looks like.

Today, I drive, and I walk, and I look, and I stare; and I shake my head in disgust, in disbelief, and in shame.

Then I begin to cry.

I cry, because we have somehow lost our way.

❋

Please re-introduce your children and grandchildren,
To the many wonders of nature, before it's much too late.

Take them hiking, fishing, or boating;
Take them to a prairie, a mountain top,
A wilderness lake, a deep pine forest,
An arid desert, the ocean's sandy shore,
Or even, to your very own backyard.

Take Them To a Wondrous Place,
Where the Joyously Wild and Free,
Red Winged Blackbird Still Sings.